D0664700

Dive

Into Living Water

by

Laurie Polich

DIVE INTO LIVING WATER:
50 DEVOTIONS FOR TEENS ON THE GOSPEL OF JOHN

COPYRIGHT ©2001 BY DIMENSIONS FOR LIVING

All rights reserved.
With the exception of those items so noted, no part of this work may be
reproduced or transmitted in any form or by any means, electronic or
mechanical, including photocopying and recording, or by any information
storage or retrieval system, except as may be expressly permitted by the 1976
Copyright Act or in writing from the publisher. Requests for permission
should be addressed to Dimensions for Living, 201 Eighth Avenue South,
Nashville, TN 37202.

This book is printed on acid-free, recycled paper.

ISBN 0687-05223-8

Scripture quotations marked (NIV) are taken from HOLY BIBLE, NEW
INTERNATIONAL VERSION®. NIV®. Copyright © 1973, 1978, 1984
by International Bible Society. Used by permission of Zondervan Publishing
House. All rights reserved.

Scripture quotations marked (NRSV) are taken from the New Revised
Standard Version of the Bible, copyright 1989, Division of Christian
Education of the National Council of Churches of Christ in the United
States of America. Used by permission. All rights reserved.

03 04 05 06 07 08 09 10 11— 12 11 10 9 8 7 6 5

MANUFACTURED IN THE UNITED STATES OF AMERICA

Contents

Introduction 9

In the Beginning
(John 1:1-18) 10

Being a Signpost
(John 1:19-34) 12

Follow Me
(John 1:35-51) 14

Life of the Party
(John 2:1-12) 16

Cleaning House
(John 2:13-25) 18

Born Again
(John 3:1-16) 20

Turn on the Light
(John 3:17-21) 22

Stepping Aside
(John 3:22-36) 24

Facing the Truth
(John 4:1-26) 26

Sharing the Truth
(John 4:27-42) 28

Faith and Belief
(John 4:43-54) 30

Do You Want to Get Well?
(John 5:1-15) 32

Like Father, Like Son
(John 5:16-30) 34

Weighing the Evidence
(John 5:31-47) 36

Come and Get It
(John 6:1-14) 38

Walking on Water
(John 6:15-22) 40

Bread of Life
(John 6:23-59) 42

Counting the Cost
(John 6:60-71) 44

Not Yet Time
(John 7:1-13) 46

Right Judgment
(John 7:14-31) 48

Living Water
(John 7:32-39) 50

Who Is This Man?
(John 7:40-53) 52

Pointing the Finger
(John 8:1-11) 54

Light of the World
(John 8:12-30) 56

Freedom and Slavery
(John 8:31-47) 58

The God of the Present
(John 8:48-59) 60

Grace and Healing
(John 9:1-15) 62

Eyes to See
(John 9:16-41) 64

The Good Shepherd
(John 10:1-21) 66

One With the Father
(John 10:22-42) 68

God's Timing
(John 11:1-22) 70

Back From the Dead
(John 11:23-57) 72

Scandalous Love
(John 12:1-11) 74

The Audience of One
(John 12:12-26) 76

The Time to Decide
(John 12:27-50) 78

Servant Leadership
(John 13:1-17) 80

Tests of Loyalty
(John 13:18-38) 82

One Way to God
(John 14:1-14) 84

Comforter and Counselor
(John 14:15-31) 86

The Vine and the Branches
(John 15:1-27) 88

Pain That Brings Joy
(John 16:1-33) 90

Jesus' Prayer
(John 17:1-26) 92

Peter's Denial
(John 18:1-27) 94

Pilate's Dilemma
(John 18:28-40) 96

Sentenced Without a Crime
(John 19:1-16) 98

The Suffering of Christ
(John 19:17-42) 100

He's Alive!
(John 20:1-18) 102

The Need for Evidence
(John 20:19-31) 104

Resurrection Meal
(John 21:1-14) 106

Feed My Sheep
(John 21:15-25) 108

Dedication

For Synicka Nash
May she never forget who she is—
a child of God.
And may she always know
how much she is loved.

Acknowledgments

Special thanks to:
Earl Palmer, whose insights color each page;
and
C. S. Lewis, whose quotations present deep truths
in simple ways.

Introduction

Y ou are about to dive into an adventure. But it's a different kind of adventure. It's an adventure into your soul. You will get as much out of it as you put into it. You can take a shallow dive and let these words skim the surface of your life. Or you can dive deeply and allow the words to penetrate your heart.

It's kind of like the difference between snorkeling and scuba diving. When you snorkel, you put on a mask and fins and skim along the top of the ocean, gazing at whatever fish happen to swim by. Scuba diving is a lot more work—but you get to see a lot more fish. The adventure is greater if you're willing to pay the price.

Life is like that: The things that are the most rewarding require the most work. So the way you approach this book will make all the difference. Let me give you a few hints:

- You will notice that I've included Scripture verses at the top of each devotional. These are the verses that pertain to that devotional. As much as I hope you'll read my words, it's more important that you read God's Word. So don't skip the verses or you'll skip the most important part of this book.
- You will also notice as you read the printed verses that not all the Scripture is included, so you will get more out of the devotional if you have your Bible with you. Think of it as scuba equipment. (And it's not nearly as heavy as a tank.)
- Finally, there are questions at the end of each devotional that will help you dive even deeper into God's Word. These questions will help you understand the words you are reading and reflect on how God is using those words to speak to your life.

That's the real miracle of God's Word. Though the Bible was written centuries ago, its words are applicable for today. And whether you've been a Christian for awhile or you're just at the beginning of your faith, the Book of John is a great place to start.

More than any other book, John's Gospel will help you set the foundation for your relationship with God. That's what the Christian faith is—a relationship. God created you and wants to know you; the Bible is the story of this God. The Book of John is the story of God's Son; through his life, death, and resurrection, we come to know God.

But wait—I'm getting ahead of myself. Turn the next page and read the story for yourself. This is one dive you will never forget. Because the water you're about to dive into is living.

In the Beginning
John 1:1-18

In the beginning was the Word, and the Word was with God, and the Word was God. He was in the beginning with God. All things came into being through him, and without him not one thing came into being. … There was a man sent from God, whose name was John. He came as a witness to testify to the light, so that all might believe through him. … But to all who received [the Word], who believed in his name, he gave power to become children of God, … And the Word became flesh and lived among us, and we have seen his glory, the glory as of a father's only son, full of grace and truth….No one has ever seen God. It is God the only Son, who is close to the Father's heart, who has made him known. (John 1:1-3, 6-7, 12, 14, 18, NRSV)

Discover Living Water

Have you ever been to a musical? If so, you know the actors communicate by singing to each other. Two guys could be fighting and suddenly break into song, singing "I'm going to kiillll you" in perfect harmony. A guy and a girl may be just about to kiss, but they'll stop inches from each other's lips to sing a love song first. (I always secretly wonder if one of them has bad breath.)

Another thing that happens in a musical is at the beginning when the conductor comes out and leads the orchestra in an overture, a medley of all the songs that are going to be heard throughout the show. The overture introduces themes and hints at stories but gives away none of the details. You have to stay and see the musical for that.

The first eighteen verses of John are similar to an overture.

With the words, *In the beginning,* we are introduced to the Word of God. This Word is described as one who created all life—making him equal to God. We are told a man named John will introduce him, but not all people will understand who he is. After sixteen verses describing him, we are finally told who he is in the seventeenth verse. And with that, the curtain opens on the story of Jesus Christ.

Drink From Living Water

All the themes touched upon in these verses will expand as the Gospel unfolds. But you have to read on to see how. Many people never do. But the fact that you've picked up this book and are reading these words shows you are making a different choice. And this passage is just a taste of what's to come. You are about to turn the pages on the greatest story ever told. And you're more than just the audience of this story; you're part of it.

Verse 12 says, "But to all who received him, who believed in his name, he gave power to become children of God." This invitation to believe is our entrance in the story. Our response will determine our part. We can stay in darkness and observe God's story from afar. Or we can enter the story as children of God. All we have to do is see Jesus for who he really is—and believe.

"No one has ever seen God. It is God the only Son, who is close to the Father's heart, who has made him known" (John 1:18). Keep reading and you'll see how.

Dive Into Living Water

① Jesus is first introduced as "the Word." What do you think that means?

Why is Jesus called that?

② Verse 10 says, "He was in the world, and the world came into being through him; yet the world did not know him." What does this tell you about who Jesus is?

What does it tell you about who people think Jesus is?

Do you find this to be true in the people around you?

③ What does verse 12 say about what it means to become a child of God?

Do you consider yourself a child of God?

Why or why not?

Being a Signpost
John 1:19–34

Now this was John's testimony when the Jews of Jerusalem sent priests and Levites to ask him who he was. ...

John replied in the words of Isaiah the prophet, "I am the voice of one calling in the desert, 'Make straight the way for the Lord.'"

Now some Pharisees who had been sent questioned him, "Why then do you baptize if you are not the Christ, nor Elijah, nor the Prophet?"

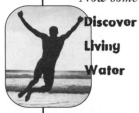

Discover Living Water

"I baptize with water," John replied, "but among you stands one you do not know. He is the one who comes after me, the thongs of whose sandals I am not worthy to untie." (John 1:19, 23-34, NIV)

Have you ever been to Las Vegas? It's a city filled with bright lights and neon signs. Some of the signs are so captivating you could spend your whole night staring at them instead of actually going to the places they advertise. The only problem is that the whole reason the signs exist is to lead you to those places. So unless you get past the sign, the sign hasn't done its job.

As Christians, we are supposed to be like signposts. Our job is to point people to Jesus Christ. John the Baptist shows us how it's done in this passage. It must have been tempting for John to keep people attracted to himself instead of pointing them toward Jesus. Many of John's followers thought he was the Messiah. But John never faltered for a moment. He knew his job was to be a signpost—and he pointed the way for people to get to the real Messiah, Jesus Christ.

Being a signpost requires that you be attention-getting enough for people to see you but not so attention-getting that people never move past you. John definitely falls in the "attention-getting" category.

Drink From Living Water

He ran around the wilderness eating locusts and honey, yelling to the crowds, "Repent and be baptized!" (see Matthew 3 for details). But with all the attention he was getting, John didn't let people stay focused on him. Instead, he put the focus on Jesus.

When a sign attracts too much attention, people can get caught up looking at it instead of going where the sign's directing them.

The same thing can happen with Christians. If people focus on us instead of looking through us to Jesus Christ, we aren't really doing our jobs. We want people to get past us to the Savior they really need.

What kind of signpost are you? Most of us either attract too much attention (by being a "good person" and never letting anyone know why) or too little attention (by not being any different at all). We can learn from John the Baptist. A good sign directs people where they need to go.

① Read the Scripture passage again. What stands out to you about John the Baptist? Why?

② If you had to describe the kind of sign you are as a Christian, would you be big or small? bright or hard to see? What words or pictures would be on your sign? What evidence of God would people see when they looked at you? Describe yourself in the space below or draw a sign that represents you.

③ Do you struggle more with being the kind of sign that attracts people by standing out (and not telling people why) or being the kind of sign that doesn't stand out at all (because you have trouble living out your faith)?

Write a prayer to God about the kind of sign you want to be. Ask God for the strength to be the kind of witness God can use to bring other people to Jesus.

Follow Me
John 1:35–51

When Jesus turned and saw them following, he said to them, "What are you looking for?" They said to him, "Rabbi" (which translated means Teacher), "where are you staying?" He said to them, "Come and see." They came and saw where he was staying, and they remained with him that day. It was about four o'clock in the afternoon. One of the two who heard John speak and followed him was Andrew, Simon Peter's brother. He first found his brother Simon and said to him, "We have found the Messiah" (which is translated Anointed). He brought Simon to Jesus, who looked at him and said, "You are Simon son of John. You are to be called Cephas" (which is translated Peter). The next day Jesus decided to go to Galilee. He found Philip and said to him, "Follow me." (John 1:38-43, NRSV)

Discover Living Water

When Jesus approaches his disciples for the first time, he says, "Follow me." He doesn't give them a map or a schedule. He doesn't consult them about their plans. Instead he invites them to become a part of his schedule and conform themselves to his plans. That's what it means to be a follower of Jesus Christ.

When I was in junior high, my friends and I used bungee chords to tie our books to the back of our bikes. But there's another way to use bungee cords. People tie them to their bodies and jump off very high places. I can remember thinking, *I'd never do that—it's just stupid.* But the truth was, it scared me to death.

One day my youth group was at an amusement park, and two guys in the group decided to bungee jump. I went along to videotape their adventure. On the way there one of them said, "Laurie, I dare you to try it." (I hate it when that happens.) I hoped that once we arrived, the people who worked at the bungee jumping place would talk me out of it. Instead by the time they were finished, they convinced me it was the safest possible thing I could do with my body. It was only after I reluctantly agreed that they pulled out a ten-page document for me to sign that said (in very fine print) if I did happen to die, they were not responsible. Needless to say, I was terrified when I attached my ropes and began my climb.

After I got to the top, there was a guy who proceeded to give me a pep talk. He said,

Drink From Living Water

"You can be as creative as you want with your jump." I was not interested in creativity. I was interested in staying alive. So I went with the very creative "step off the platform with your eyes closed" jump. Everything was in slow motion. Finally the moment came when the rope held me, and I started bouncing up the other way. I let out the biggest scream you ever heard. "WOOHOO, I'M ALIVE!!!!!"

Never in all my days of using bungee cords to hold my books did I ever let out a scream like that. But when my body was attached to one, I had a very different relationship with that bungee cord. My life was in its hands.

When Jesus says, "Follow me," he is telling us to put our lives in his hands. He is not asking for our Sundays; he is asking for all our days. He is not asking if he can follow us; he is asking if we want to follow him. Those willing to take this risk will find the terrifying joy of jumping into life with the ropes of Jesus around them. And they will experience the freedom and exhilaration of what it really means to be alive.

Dive Into Living Water

① Many believe in Jesus; few follow him. Would you describe yourself as a believer or a follower? Why?

② On the scale below, place yourself according to how much of your life you've given to Jesus. Are you satisfied with where you are on the scale? If not, where would you like to be?

nothing   some things   most things   everything

③ What specific areas of your life do you have the hardest time giving to Jesus? What steps could you take to give Jesus those things? Are you willing to take those steps? If so, pray that God will help you release whatever it is you struggle with and follow Jesus.

Life of the Party

John 2:1-12

Nearby stood six stone water jars, the kind used by the Jews for ceremonial washing, each holding from twenty to thirty gallons.

Jesus said to the servants, "Fill the jars with water"; so they filled them to the brim.

Then he told them, "Now draw some out and take it to the master of the banquet."

Discover Living Water

They did so, and the master of the banquet tasted the water that had been turned into wine. He did not realize where it had come from, though the servants who had drawn the water knew. Then he called the bridegroom aside and said, "Everyone brings out the choice wine first and then the cheaper wine after the guests have had too much to drink; but you have saved the best till now." (John 2:6-10, NIV)

I magine Jesus at a party. Where do you picture him? Maybe you see him leading a Bible study over in the corner. Or standing with some of your friends giving a sermon on partying. Probably the last place you'd imagine Jesus is by the sink, quietly changing the tap water into fine wine. But that's where we find him in this story.

In this passage we see a side of Jesus that surprises many Christians. (It's a great story to share with some of your non-Christian friends.) But it also says something important about the satisfaction only Jesus can provide.

At this time in Jewish history, wedding feasts were huge parties that lasted several days. Jesus, Jesus' mother, and the disciples had all come to this particular celebration; and when the wine ran out, Jesus' mother came over to tell Jesus.

It was clear from Jesus' response that he had no intention of doing anything at this party that would make him stand out. But it turned out to be the setting of his first miracle. Out of the water used for washing, he created a wine superior to all the other wine served at the party.

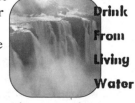

Drink From Living Water

The significance of this miracle is the kind of wine Jesus provides. The party guests were happy with their less superior wine because they had never had anything better. Sometimes we find ourselves in that same boat. We think fulfillment is found by stuffing ourselves with food, drinking alcohol, or experimenting with sex. But these things only satisfy us for awhile—and if we keep indulging in them, we're left with an eating disorder, an addiction, or a broken heart, feeling emptier than before.

Many people spend their whole lives convinced that if they keep filling their stomachs with their immediate cravings, they'll find the satisfaction their hearts seek. But they never do. Instead their desires get deeper, while their "fixes" (from alcohol, food, or sex) just feel cheaper. And they are left with longings that are unfulfilled.

Like the wedding host says in this passage, the wine—or satisfaction we provide for ourselves—may seem choice at first but usually tastes cheap in the end. The satisfaction Jesus provides lasts forever.

❶ What things do teenagers do to get satisfaction?

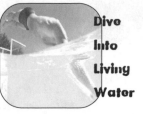

Dive Into Living Water

Which of these things are good?

Which are bad?

❷ What things do you do to get satisfaction?

Which of these things are good?

Which (if any) are bad?

❸ Are there any habits or addictions in your life that come between you and God? If so, are you ready to give them up? What would it take for you to do that?

Cleaning House
John 2:12–25

In the temple courts he found men selling cattle, sheep and doves, and others sitting at tables exchanging money. So he made a whip out of cords, and drove all from the temple area, both sheep and cattle; he scattered the coins of the money changers and overturned their tables. To those who sold doves he said, "Get these out of here! How dare you turn my Father's house into a market!" (John 2:14-16, NIV)

Discover
Living
Water

Anyone who pictures Jesus in a white robe picking flowers and skipping along the shores of Galilee will find this passage a bit disrupting. Cracking the whip and knocking down tables, Jesus shows us that some things make him really angry. And misusing God's house is one of them.

The people selling things in the Temple might not have been trying to make God mad. In fact they may have rationalized that they were doing God a favor. After all, their sales were drawing a lot of people to the Temple who normally wouldn't have come. But the sellers weren't interested in people coming to worship. They were interested in making a profit. And that's what made Jesus so angry.

Rationalizing still happens today. People do things "in the name of Jesus" that are really for personal gain. Sometimes it's to make money—like the TV evangelists who promise God's blessing to people who send them checks. Other times it's to gain power—like church leaders who subtly get people to worship them instead of God.

Drink
From
Living
Water

Both are wrong in God's eyes. And whether someone uses the church to build an income or an image, either way God is not pleased.

Many good Christians have fallen because their drives to honor God became drives for money or power instead. They (and the people around them) suffer for their sins.

Jesus knew the danger of using God's gifts for personal

gain. At this point in his ministry, Jesus was very popular, and he could have used his status to bolster his ministry. But Jesus never gave in to the popularity he had from the people. He knew that human power is fleeting—that the only lasting power is from God.

From this passage we see that the only thing to be worshiped in God's house is God. If we're worshiping anything else, we can expect at some point that the "tables will fly." It's Jesus' way of cleaning house.

❶ What examples have you seen of people abusing money or power in the name of Christ?

Have you (or anyone you know) ever been affected by it?

❷ Why do you think Jesus was so angry in this passage?

What kinds of things do you think would make Jesus angry today?

❸ What evidence does Christ give for his death and resurrection in this passage?

How do you think people understood Jesus then? How do we understand him now?

Born Again
John 3:1-16

Now there was a man of the Pharisees named Nicodemus, a member of the Jewish ruling council. He came to Jesus at night and said, "Rabbi, we know you are a teacher who has come from God. For no one could perform the miraculous signs you are doing if God were not with him."

Discover Living Water

In reply Jesus declared, "I tell you the truth, no one can see the kingdom of God unless he is born again."

"How can a man be born when he is old?" Nicodemus asked. "Surely he cannot enter a second time into his mother's womb to be born!"

Jesus answered, "I tell you the truth, no one can enter the kingdom of God unless he is born of water and the Spirit. Flesh gives birth to flesh, but the Spirit gives birth to spirit."
(John 3:1-6, NIV)

Nicodemus was a religious man. Not only was he a Pharisee (which was a group of strict Law-keeping Jews), but he was also a leader of the church. It's safe to say most people would describe Nicodemus as a person who knew God. Except, maybe, Nicodemus.

In this passage, Nicodemus discovers the difference between *knowing about* God and *knowing* God. It was a humbling lesson for him to learn. I can remember when I learned that lesson myself.

Like Nicodemus, I thought I understood what it meant to know God. But my senior year I went to a Christian camp for the very spiritual reason that my boyfriend was going to the camp—and I wanted to be with him. That weekend I heard something I'd never heard before: God wanted to have a relationship with me. I learned faith wasn't about religion; it was about inviting Jesus into my heart. That's what it meant to be "born again." Though it was humbling for me to admit, I knew I had never done that.

I can remember standing up to receive

Drink From Living Water

Jesus' offer of new life in my heart. I made my friend stand up with me. (She was already a Christian, but I was too embarrassed to stand up alone.) It was scary because I had to admit in front of all my friends that I had never received Christ. But that day he came in—and I have never been the same.

In this passage, Nicodemus finds out that no matter how much knowledge he has about

God, in order to know God, he must be born again. Becoming a Christian can happen no other way.

No amount of "good works" can ever achieve that relationship. It's a gift. God has done the work; our job is to receive it. John 3:16 shows us how: "For God so loved the world that he gave his only Son, so that everyone who believes in him may not perish but may have eternal life."

① When you hear the phrase, *born again*, what comes to your mind? Why?

Dive Into Living Water

② How does this passage help you understand what it means to be born again?

③ Look at the analogy Jesus gives about the wind in verse 8. How does that help us to understand what it means to be born of the Spirit?

Turn on the Light
John 3:17-21

"Indeed, God did not send the Son into the world to condemn the world, but in order that the world might be saved through him. Those who believe in him are not condemned; but those who do not believe are condemned already, because they have not believed in the name of the only Son of God. And this is the judgment, that the light has come into the world, and people loved darkness rather than light because their deeds were evil. For all who do evil hate the light and do not come to the light, so that their deeds may not be exposed. But those who do what is true come to the light, so that it may be clearly seen that their deeds have been done in God." (John 3:17-21, NRSV)

Discover Living Water

Drink From Living Water

Have you ever noticed it's easier to sin when it's dark? Think about it. Let's say you're on a date with someone you really like. You come home and sit on the couch "to talk." Chances are if the light's a little bright, one of you will reach up and turn it off. And that's where the trouble begins.

If you decided to sneak out of your house, when would you do it? Probably at night. You don't see many teenagers climbing out of their windows in the middle of the day. And have you noticed that more crimes are committed at night? That drugs are often exchanged in dark alleys? That bars are kept unusually dim?

Jesus says that people love darkness instead of light when their deeds are evil. Maybe that's because you can't really see what you're doing. If you want to change the mood of a room, switch on the lights. Things look different when the view is crystal clear.

Jesus says, "All who do evil hate the light and do not come to the light, so that their deeds may not be exposed" (verse 20). That's the effect light has. If you want to experience this, take a trip to your basement. Switch on the light. Depending on how long it's been, you may see cockroaches or mice scurrying off to hide. Empty spider webs may fill the corners of the room. Perhaps holes are burrowed in the boxes you've stored. There is evidence that a whole world exists in the darkness, and it changed when you turned on the light.

Jesus had this same effect. He

was the Light that came into the world, and he found a lot of people living in the darkness. He offered them the choice to come into the light, but they had to be willing to live truthfully and openly—and not hide anymore.

God doesn't demand us to be perfect. We can never achieve that. God offers to bring us into the light, so that our cobwebs can be cleaned and our holes can be patched up. Then out of those cleaned cobwebs and patched-up holes we begin to shine as a testimony to God's power.

If you let Christ into the basement of your soul, he will do all the housecleaning. All you have to do is come into the light.

① What would you describe as "deeds of darkness"?

Dive Into Living Water

What deeds of darkness have you seen your friends do?

Is it hard for you not to do them?

② Would you say you live mostly in the light (being open and honest) or mostly in the dark (hiding your deeds)?

③ Do specific areas of your life need a little housecleaning? If so, what are they?

Stepping Aside
John 3:22-36

They came to John and said to him, "Rabbi, the one who was with you across the Jordan, to whom you testified, here he is baptizing, and all are going to him." John answered, "No one can receive anything except what has been given from heaven. You yourselves are my witnesses that I said, 'I am not the Messiah, but I have been sent ahead of him.' He who has the bride is the bridegroom. The friend of the bridegroom, who stands and hears him, rejoices greatly at the bridegroom's voice. For this reason my joy has been fulfilled. He must increase, but I must decrease."
(John 3:26-30, NRSV)

Discover Living Water

Imagine you are at a wedding and the bride is making her entrance. She walks down the aisle and instead of being met by her groom, she stands face-to-face with the best man, who is standing in front of the groom waving to the crowd. It wouldn't take long for everyone to realize that the best man had a little ego problem. (Unless he had a crush on the bride and figured this was his chance.) Either way, most people would agree that the best man was not doing his job.

In this passage, Jesus is described as a bridegroom and John the Baptist is the best man. Unlike the scenario just described, John the Baptist doesn't ever steal the spotlight from Jesus. He keeps the attention where it belongs. At this point in the story, people were beginning to be baptized by Jesus instead of John, and

John could have felt threatened by that. But he rests secure in his role as the best man, and he is not swayed by his own ego needs.

Too often Christian speakers, pastors, and musicians shift the focus from Christ to themselves.

Drink From Living Water

They start out doing ministry "in the name of the Lord," and soon their own names are being glorified instead. T-shirts are printed, posters are made, and usually it's not Christ's image blazoned across them. Many of us add to the problem by buying the posters and wearing the shirts, advertising their images ourselves.

John's statement about being a friend to the bridegroom and not being the bridegroom himself stands as a warning to Christians today—particularly those who find themselves on some kind of stage. The stage in heaven looks different from the stage on earth; and those who glorify God, rather than themselves, are the ones who are on the heavenly stage.

John the Baptist experiences fulfillment in being the bridegroom's friend. That's the way it should be for us. When we try to steal the focus from the bridegroom, we find that we are a disappointment to everyone, including ourselves. Because ultimately it's the real bridegroom people want to see.

Especially the bride.

❶ When John says a person can receive only what is given from heaven (verse 27), what do you think he means?

Dive Into Living Water

❷ What is John's attitude about being best man to Christ (verse 29)?

How is this an example to us?

❸ In verse 30, John says that Jesus must increase, while he must decrease. What would it take for Jesus to become greater in your life?

Facing the Truth
John 4:1-26

Jesus said to her, "Everyone who drinks of this water will be thirsty again, but those who drink of the water that I will give them will never be thirsty. The water that I will give will become in them a spring of water gushing up to eternal life." The woman said to him, "Sir, give me this water, so that I may never be thirsty or have to keep coming here to draw water."

Discover Living Water

Jesus said to her, "Go, call your husband, and come back." The woman answered him, "I have no husband." Jesus said to her, "You are right in saying, 'I have no husband'; for you have had five husbands, and the one you have now is not your husband. What you have said is true!" (John 4:13-18, NRSV)

We all have secrets. The woman in this story did too. That's why she came to get water in the middle of the day. She wanted to pick a time when no one would be there so she could do her business and slip out of sight. But her plan was ruined when she ran into Jesus. At first she was probably relieved; Jewish men never spoke to Samaritan women. But this Jewish man was different, and he initiated a conversation that changed her life.

They started off talking about water, when suddenly the subject changed. Out of nowhere, Jesus said the dreaded words that threatened to expose her secret, "Go call your husband and come back." Jesus knew she didn't have a husband. But he also knew she needed to face the truth about her life.

This woman had tried to find love in all the wrong places. Maybe you can relate to that. She wasn't proud of her choices, but she had gotten caught in a pattern she couldn't change. After five failed marriages, she was in her sixth relation- ship—

Drink From Living Water

sleeping with a man she wasn't married to. When Jesus confronted her, she must have felt embarrassed and scared. But Jesus didn't challenge her to humiliate her. He did it to set her free. By helping her recognize her thirst, Jesus opened her heart to receive the living water she craved.

In many ways we are like that woman. We get involved in bad habits and bad relationships and then have a tendency to hide. We stay away from church, avoid Christian friends, lie to our families, and sometimes even lie to ourselves. But deep in our hearts we long to be found. The Samaritan woman didn't know this would be the day she would be found. But that's exactly what happened. After Jesus exposed her secret, he offered her the kind of satisfaction she had never found with all those men. From that point on, she could be free to live openly without shame or guilt.

Our secrets may keep us from God—but they don't keep God from us. No matter what you've done or where you've been, God's desire is for you to "get found." Because only when you stop hiding and face the truth, can you truly be set free.

Dive Into Living Water

❶ Put yourself in the Samaritan woman's place. What would Jesus say to you if he bumped into you today?

❷ Do you ever hide things from God? How about others? If so, what do you hide? Why do you hide these things?

❸ After reading this story, is there anything you feel God wants you to face in your life in order to make a change? If so, are you ready to face it? What steps will you take to begin living differently?

Sharing the Truth

John 4:27–42

Then, leaving her water jar, the woman went back to the town and said to the people, "Come, see a man who told me everything I ever did. Could this be the Christ?" They came out of the town and made their way toward him.... Many of the Samaritans from that town believed in him because of the woman's testimony, "He told me everything I ever did." So when the Samaritans came to him, they urged him to stay with them, and he stayed two days. And because of his words many more became believers.

They said to the woman, "We no longer believe just because of what you said; now we have heard for ourselves, and we know that this man really is the Savior of the world." (John 4:28-30, 39-42, NIV)

Discover Living Water

In this passage we see the results of a changed life. The woman with a shameful past now shares her story with the whole town. Her testimony helps many of the Samaritans come to know Jesus.

She left town alone to get water in the middle of the day. Now she is surrounded by people, telling her story. People who knew her must have seen the change. And she tells them it was Jesus who made all the difference.

This woman shows us that anyone can be a witness. All it takes is the willingness to share our stories. We don't have to have the perfect words, the right method, or a certain style to tell people about Christ. This woman didn't have any of those. All she said was, "Come, see a man who told me everything I ever did" (verse 29). And a bunch of them left town to see him! Maybe it was her excitement that caused people to want to know more. It's that same excitement in us that God can use to be a witness to our friends.

The beautiful thing about this woman's story is that God can  **Drink From Living Water** take our pain and turn it into our testimonies. The very secret this woman tried to hide became the story she told to others, and her testimony caused them to want to meet Jesus for themselves.

When people take the risk to tell their painful experiences, God uses their stories to bring healing. We see this truth in the life of this woman. God transformed something negative in her life into something positive in the lives of others. And God can do the same thing with us.

I'm sure this woman never dreamed she'd be telling her story to her entire town. But imagine how she felt when she heard their words: "We know that this man really is the Savior of the world" (verse 42). It was through her wounds they were healed—all because she took the risk to share her story. How many people would be changed if they heard yours?

❶ What changes do you observe in the woman as her story progresses?

What do you think made the difference?

❷ Have you ever shared your testimony with anyone? If so, how did it go? If not, why not?

❸ Write in the space below what you would say to someone about your experience with Jesus. Then write the names of three people with whom you would like to be able to share your faith.

Faith and Belief

John 4:43–54

Once more he visited Cana in Galilee, where he had turned the water into wine. And there was a certain royal official whose son lay sick at Capernaum. When this man heard that Jesus had arrived in Galilee from Judea, he went to him and begged him to come and heal his son, who was close to death.

"Unless you people see miraculous signs and wonders," Jesus told him, "you will never believe."

The royal official said, "Sir, come down before my child dies."

Jesus replied, "You may go. Your son will live."

The man took Jesus at his word and departed.

(John 4:46-50, NIV)

Discover Living Water

At first glance, Jesus' response to the royal official seems rather cold. But it shows us the importance of faith. Like a muscle, our faith needs to be exercised in order to grow. This passage shows that Jesus wants this growth to happen.

After the official makes his desperate request, Jesus responds by saying, "Unless you people see miraculous signs and wonders, you will never believe" (verse 48). It's clear by Jesus' tone that he is seeking a deeper faith for the official and his household.

This man has an agenda for how he wants Jesus to work in his life. He wants him to heal his son. There's nothing wrong with his request; but Jesus' response shows that he has another, equally important agenda for this man. He tells him to go—that his son has been healed. At that moment the man has to decide whether or not he can take Jesus at his word.

The man knows he might not be able to find Jesus again. What if his son isn't healed? But Jesus is asking him to believe in the  unknown before he can be assured by the known—because that's what produces faith. When the man takes Jesus at his word, he not only experiences his son's healing, but he also experiences his own growth of faith. And that's what Jesus wanted most.

Too often our prayers are consumed with asking God to change our circumstances. But this passage indicates that God is involved in a more important

Drink From Living Water

agenda: changing us. Most of our prayers involve temporary answers anyway. Though this official's son was healed, he would eventually die. We all do! But the faith that was produced by the healing had an eternal purpose—bringing the man and his household to everlasting life in Christ. That was what mattered most.

In this passage Jesus shows us that he can and will do miracles in our lives. But our faith is not to be based on miracles; it's to be based on the one who does the miracles. That's the foundation on which we're to stand. It's the only foundation secure enough to hold our faith.

Dive Into Living Water

❶ How do you think this man felt when he asked Jesus to heal his son? When Jesus responded the way he did in verse 48?

How would you have felt?

❷ When Jesus tells the man that his son has been healed, the man believes Jesus. Would you have done the same thing? Would you have left believing it had happened or hoping it had happened? What does this passage teach you about trusting God?

❸ How much do you trust God with your needs and concerns? Do you believe God always answers your prayers, sometimes answers your prayers, or never answers your prayers? What would it take for you to trust God more?

Do You Want to Get Well?
John 5:1–15

Now there is in Jerusalem near the Sheep Gate a pool, which in Aramaic is called Bethesda and which is surrounded by five covered colonnades. Here a great number of disabled people used to lie—the blind, the lame, the paralyzed. One who was there had been an invalid for thirty-eight years. When Jesus saw him lying there and learned that he had been in this condition for a long time, he asked him, "Do you want to get well?"

"Sir," the invalid replied, "I have no one to help me into the pool when the water is stirred. While I am trying to get in, someone else goes down ahead of me."

Then Jesus said to him, "Get up! Pick up your mat and walk." At once the man was cured; he picked up his mat and walked. The day on which this took place was a Sabbath. (John 5:2-9, NIV)

Discover Living Water

Some of my fondest childhood memories are of the days I stayed home sick. I could sleep in, not do my chores, watch TV, and be waited on by my mom. The only bad part about it was being sick!

I can remember sometimes trying to fake it. If I had a tiny sore throat or stuffed-up nose, I tried to make it seem much more serious. (That's when I first got interested in acting.) Most of the time my attempt didn't work—my mom was really smart. But when it did, those were the best days of all. I wished I could have stayed in bed forever!

Of course if I did, I never would have gotten through school. And I never would have gone to college. I never would have gotten a job. I might still be in my bed, relying on my mom to take care of me—all because I never would have learned to take responsibility for myself.

The man in this story is a little like that. True, he had a disability. At first glance it seemed he couldn't do anything about it.

Drink From Living Water

When Jesus asks him if he wants to get healed, it seems like a ridiculous question. The interesting thing is that the man doesn't answer yes! Instead, he goes on and on about why he hasn't gotten healed—and how it's everyone's fault but his. He can't get to the water because no one will help him. Everyone else gets there first. Yet he continues to stay in that place for thirty-eight years. Why?

As a victim, this man does not have to take responsibility for his life. If he found a way to get

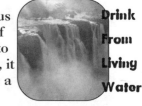

to the pool, you would think he could find a way into the pool—or at least away from the pool if he couldn't get in. But the man stays right where he is, convincing himself he can't do anything else. Then Jesus asks him in verse 6, "Do you want to get well?"

The great news about this story is that Jesus can break through and bring healing, even when people aren't sure they want to be healed. While the man is talking, Jesus interrupts his excuses and says, "Get up!" (verse 8). And he does!

After two days of waiting on me in bed, my mom said that to me too. And twenty years later, I'm glad I did.

❶ Do you think this man wanted to get well?

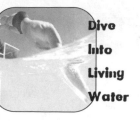

Dive
Into
Living
Water

Why or why not?

❷ How do you think this man felt when Jesus said, "Get up"?

Do you think he was afraid? surprised? angry?

How would you have felt?

❸ Is there anything in your life that you feel God wants to heal or change?

If so, what? Would you be ready if God wanted to take care of it today?

Like Father, Like Son
John 5:16-30

Discover Living Water

So, because Jesus was doing these things on the Sabbath, the Jews persecuted him. Jesus said to them, "My Father is always at his work to this very day, and I, too, am working." For this reason the Jews tried all the harder to kill him; not only was he breaking the Sabbath, but he was even calling God his own Father, making himself equal with God. ...

"I tell you the truth, whoever hears my word and believes him who sent me has eternal life and will not be condemned; he has crossed over from death to life." (John 5:16-18, 24, NIV)

My brother was named after my father: Tyrone Theodore Polich, Jr., but everyone calls him "Chip." He was given this nickname because he was supposed to be a "chip off the old block"—a junior version of my dad. And his name bears testimony to that fact. In this passage, Jesus reveals that in a sense, he, too, is a "chip off the old block." But he has some trouble convincing the Jews, since he claimed that his father was God.

The Jews were upset with Jesus because he had healed a man on the Sabbath; and according to the law, no work was to be done on that day. Jesus explains that he did this because he was following his father's footsteps; and since his father continued to work on the Sabbath, Jesus did too. The Jews knew that God was the only one who continued

working on the Sabbath, so they realized that Jesus was calling God his father. This made them very angry. (A slight understatement since verse 18 says they tried to kill him.)

In 1 Peter 2:6, Jesus is called the "chosen and precious cornerstone" to

Drink From Living Water

which the Scriptures point. But 1 Peter 2:7 goes on to say that this stone will be rejected and will become a stumbling block to those who do not believe. In this passage, Jesus experiences this rejection because he claims to be God's Son. Nevertheless, Jesus stands by his claim; and the Jews are forced to decide whether or not they believe him.

Many people have called Jesus a great prophet, teacher,

and healer. But they've stopped short of calling him God's Son. This passage makes it clear that in order to accept Jesus, we must accept him as he is—because it is our belief in Jesus as God's Son that leads us to eternal life (verse 24).

If ever there was a "chip off the old block," it was—and is—Jesus Christ. Whether or not we accept him is our choice. The decision we make determines whether this "chip" will become our cornerstone or stumbling block. More importantly, it will determine whether we dismiss him as a prophet or follow him as Lord.

① According to this passage, what privileges has the Father given Jesus?

Which ones show he is God's Son?

② Can we believe in the Father without believing in the Son? Why or why not?

③ Jesus makes some amazing claims in this passage. Do you have trouble understanding anything Jesus says? If so, with whom could you talk to better understand Jesus' claims? Write down that person's name and decide when you will talk with him or her about it.

Weighing the Evidence
John 5:31-47

"You have sent to John and he has testified to the truth. Not that I accept human testimony; but I mention it that you may be saved. John was a lamp that burned and gave light, and you chose for a time to enjoy his light.

"I have testimony weightier than that of John. For the very work that the Father has given me to finish, and which I am doing, testifies that the Father has sent me. And the Father who sent me has himself testified concerning me. You have never heard his voice nor seen his form, nor does his word dwell in you, for you do not believe the one he sent. You diligently study the Scriptures because you think that by them you possess eternal life. These are the Scriptures that testify about me, yet you refuse to come to me to have life." (John 5:33-40, NIV)

Discover Living Water

One of the most famous trials in recent history was the O. J. Simpson trial. People stayed glued to their televisions listening to testimonies of what happened on the night of the crime. The reliability of the testimony was directly proportionate to the reliability of the witness, and very few witnesses proved to be reliable as the trial wore on.

I can remember watching some witnesses change their testimonies, depending on the effect their answers had on their popularity. The quest for fame became more important than the search for truth, leaving everyone feeling that the truth was never heard—even after the verdict came in.

In this passage we find Jesus on trial, as he faces the judgment of the Jews. Jesus needs reliable witnesses to prove he is God's Son, so he brings four of them to the stand. First he brings John the Baptist, calling him "a lamp that gave light" to the truth. When we look at John's testimony in chapter 1, it's clear John believed Jesus was God's Son. Second, Jesus points to his own actions to prove the Father sent him (verse 36). Third, Jesus says the Father also testifies that he's God's Son. Matthew 3:17 records that when Jesus was baptized, a voice from heaven said, "This is my Son, whom I love; with him I am well pleased" (see also Luke 3:22). Finally, Jesus points to the Scriptures, saying they proclaim that he is the one

Drink From Living Water

God sent (verses 38-39). Yet the Jews still seem unwilling to see the truth.

Jesus produces four witnesses that testify to the truth of his identity. But the Jews don't believe him. Do we? Just like the O. J. trial, the verdict depends on the people's response. Was O. J. guilty? There are two different answers depending on whom you talk to. But only one of them is true.

Is Jesus God's Son? There are two answers depending on whom you talk to. But only one of them is true.

Dive Into Living Water

❶ Which of Jesus' four testimonies is the most convincing in proving to you that he is God's Son? Why?

❷ If people asked you to prove Jesus was the Son of God, how would you try to convince them?

❸ If you were called to the stand to speak about how Christ has shown himself to be true in your life, what would your testimony be?

Come and Get It

John 6:1–14

When he looked up and saw a large crowd coming toward him, Jesus said to Philip, "Where are we to buy bread for these people to eat?" He said this to test him, for he himself knew what he was going to do.

Philip answered him, "Six months' wages would not buy enough bread for each of them to get a little."

Discover Living Water

One of his disciples, Andrew, Simon Peter's brother, said to him, "There is a boy here who has five barley loaves and two fish. But what are they among so many people?" Jesus said, "Make the people sit down." Now there was a great deal of grass in the place; so they sat down, about five thousand in all. Then Jesus took the loaves, and when he had given thanks, he distributed them to those who were seated; so also the fish, as much as they wanted. (John 6:5-11, NRSV)

The feeding of the five thousand is the only miracle recorded in all four Gospels. But there is one detail that only John includes. It's a detail we don't want to miss.

By the way Jesus sets up this miracle, clearly he has some lessons to teach the disciples. First, Jesus asks Philip where he thinks they should buy bread. Since Philip was the most familiar with the area (he was from a nearby town called Bethsaida), it was appropriate for Jesus to ask him. But Philip doesn't answer the question, probably because he can't believe Jesus is asking it! Thousands of people need to be fed. If Philip had worked out the math in his head, he would have figured out they couldn't possibly come up with enough bread to feed them.

That's where Andrew comes in. In verse 9, he says, "There is a boy here who has five barley loaves and two fish." (I can only imagine the sarcastic responses of the disciples at this point.) Even Andrew questions his own suggestion. But it was those five loaves and two fish that Jesus used to do his miracle.

Drink From Living Water

The other Gospels (Matthew 14, Mark 6, Luke 9) record that the disciples found the loaves and fish, but they leave out where they found them. Only John records that they came from a small boy. Imagine for a moment how this boy must have felt. On one hand, he was chosen out of thousands of people there to participate in this great miracle. On the other hand, he had to give up his food to do it. We don't know whether

38

this was his food for one meal, one day, or one week. But his willingness to give Jesus what he had is what this passage is about.

Can you imagine how the boy felt after this miracle happened? The disciples probably lifted him up on their shoulders and cheered. (And Andrew had the last laugh.) This boy, who had so little, was used by Jesus to do so much. John records this detail so we will know the story is not about how much we have but how much of it we are willing to give. And we can trust Jesus for what he is able to do with our gift.

But we can't miss the significance of how it must have felt for this little boy to let go of what he had, unsure if he would ever get it back. For that is what faith is all about.

① Why did Jesus ask the disciples where they could buy bread for the people if he 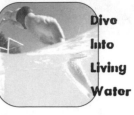 already knew he was going to feed them?

Dive Into Living Water

What was his purpose in asking them this question?

② Why do you think Jesus used what the boy had instead of just doing the miracle himself?

What does that tell you about Jesus?

③ When there is a need, do you tend to respond like Philip, Andrew, or the little boy?

How could God use something you have to meet a need right now?

Walking on Water
John 6:15-22

When evening came, his disciples went down to the lake, where they got into a boat and set off across the lake for Capernaum. By now it was dark, and Jesus had not yet joined them. A strong wind was blowing and the waters grew rough. When they had rowed three or three and a half miles, they saw Jesus approaching the boat, walking on the water; and they were terrified. But he said to them, "It is I; don't be afraid." (John 6:16-20, NIV)

Discover Living Water

I used to love slumber parties. (Although I'm not sure why they were called that since "slumber" was the one thing you didn't do.) But there is one slumber party that stands out in my memory.

My friends and I were huddled in the stairwell telling ghost stories. It was the perfect setting: The lights were off, and the doors were closed at the top and bottom of the staircase. So it was kind of like being in a closet.

One of my friends was in the middle of a really scary story and whispered, "Then the door slowly opened." Right at that moment, the door opened at the top of the stairs. We screamed and dog-piled on top of one another. When we looked up, we saw my friend's mom standing in the doorway holding a plate of cookies. She started to laugh. Then we all started to laugh. We spent the rest of the night re-enacting the story and laughing about it together.

There is something about the relief you feel after being really scared that feels really good. That's probably how the disciples felt in this

Drink From Living Water

passage. It was dark, the wind was blowing, and the waters were rough. They were all alone. Suddenly they look up to see someone walking toward them—on the water! You can imagine them clutching one another, trying to be brave but totally terrified. Then they hear a loud voice saying, "It is I; don't be afraid" (verse 20). It's Jesus! Imagine their relief. I can just hear Philip telling

Andrew afterward that he was never really scared. (It's a guy thing.)

The great thing about an incident like this is that it bonds the people who were there. My friends and I told the story of our slumber party many times, and every time we did, we would find ourselves saying, "I guess you had to be there."

This was a miracle experienced only by the disciples. The rest of Jesus's miracles were performed for others, but this one was just for them. Something tells me that every time they told the story, they would look at one another and say, "I guess you had to be there." And even though they were scared when it happened, I bet they were glad they were there.

Dive Into Living Water

❶ Have you ever been with your friends and had something really scary happen?

How did you feel after it was over?

❷ Why do you think Jesus did what he did in this passage?

What (if anything) was he trying to show the disciples about himself?

❸ When was the last time God surprised you?

How did it affect your relationship with God?

What (if anything) has happened in your life to cause you to see God in a new way?

41

Bread of Life
John 6:23-59

When they found him on the other side of the lake, they asked him, "Rabbi, when did you get here?"

Jesus answered, "I tell you the truth, you are looking for me, not because you saw miraculous signs but because you ate the loaves and had your fill. Do not work for food that spoils, but for food

Discover Living Water

that endures to eternal life, which the Son of Man will give you. On him God the Father has placed his seal of approval."

"Sir," they said, "from now on give us this bread."

Then Jesus declared, "I am the bread of life. He who comes to me will never go hungry, and he who believes in me will never be thirsty." (John 6:25-27, 34-35, NIV)

I love to eat. It's something I look forward to each day. But one thing I've realized about food (other than the fact that it has created a need for exercise in my life) is that the pleasure it provides is short-lived. Whether I stop when I'm satisfied or eat until I'm really full, I'm left feeling that food isn't all I try to make it to be. That's the lesson Jesus teaches us in this passage.

After the feeding of the five thousand, Jesus has become very popular with the people. (Apparently other people like to eat too.) A great crowd has started to follow Jesus, but he knows they are following him only because he fed them. So he makes it clear he will not give them the food they seek—because it's temporal. The food he wants to give them is eternal.

When the people ask Jesus to produce more bread, he announces that he *is* the Bread.

This response doesn't do much for his popularity. But Jesus doesn't care about being popular—what he cares about is truth. Jesus wants people to understand the bread they eat will never permanently fill them; they will always want more. This spiritual

Drink From Living Water

hunger is what makes people ready for Jesus— the only bread that will last.

So many times we think we know what we want. Then we get it, and it's not what we thought it would be. Jesus knows that about us. That's why he doesn't waste his time trying to satisfy our wants. He knows our needs—and those are the ones he seeks to satisfy. That's what this passage makes clear.

That message is not what people want to hear. The more Jesus talks, the less popular he becomes. The dialogue in this passage shows that people want Jesus on their terms. But Jesus comes on his own terms. At times he may not be what we *want* him to be, but he is always what we *need* him to be.

For a brief moment Jesus' popularity caused the people to want to make him King (verse 15). Now they're not so sure. By asserting his own lordship in this passage we learn that Jesus doesn't need to be "made" King. He already is.

❶ Why did people get so angry at Jesus in this passage?

Dive
Into
Living
Water

What did they want from him?

❷ How are the people in this passage similar to people today?

For what things do we ask God that are like the bread in this passage?

❸ How do Jesus' words in verses 54-56 help you understand what it means to take Communion?

Do any of his words change your understanding of Communion? If so, how?

Counting the Cost
John 6:60-71

Jesus said to them, "I tell you the truth, unless you eat the flesh of the Son of Man and drink his blood, you have no life in you. Whoever eats my flesh and drinks my blood has eternal life, and I will raise him up at the last day. ..."

From this time many of his disciples turned back and no longer followed him.

"You do not want to leave too, do you?" Jesus asked the Twelve.

Simon Peter answered him, "Lord, to whom shall we go? You have the words of eternal life. We believe and know that you are the Holy One of God." (John 6:53-54, 66-69, NIV)

Discover Living Water

The remaining verses of this chapter show how fickle a crowd can be. One minute they're cheering Jesus, trying to make him king. The next they are deserting him—for not being the king they wanted. Now Jesus is left with the faithful few who are his true friends.

The story reminds me of what happens at a big sporting event when everything rests on the final play. If the football player catches the touchdown pass, he's cheered as the game's hero. If he drops it, he walks off alone. He's met in the locker room by an obnoxious TV sportscaster who thrusts a microphone in his face and asks him how he feels. When he emerges from the locker room, he finds out who his true friends are.

In this passage Jesus finds out who his real friends are. After he has disappointed the crowd,

he is left with his disciples. Now they have to decide whether they will follow Jesus—not as the Lord they want him to be but as the Lord he is.

At times we are disappointed with God, and we have to decide the same thing. Imagine how the disciples felt **Drink From Living Water** in this passage. They have seen Jesus feed five thousand people, walk on water, and draw huge crowds. Now Jesus gives some teaching that is hard for them to hear.

Jesus says, "Whoever eats my flesh and drinks my blood has eternal life" (verse 54). We know he's speaking figuratively, and we associate his words with Communion. But the disciples didn't know that then. As the crowd grumbled and walked away, the disciples were left with the final question of faith. Would they hold on to Jesus in spite of their feelings of uncertainty? Will we?

Peter answers for those of us who do when he says, "Lord, to whom shall we go? You have the words of eternal life" (verse 68). That simple statement of faith helps us to hold on no matter how things may seem. In time we'll see things from an eternal perspective. And we will be glad we held on to Christ.

❶ Look at verse 66. Why do you think people turned back and stopped following Jesus?

Dive Into Living Water

If you were there, what do you think you would have done?

❷ Have you ever been tempted to turn away from Christ? If so, why?

❸ Do you feel the way Peter does in verse 68?

Would you continue to follow Christ even if he disappointed you? Why or why not?

Not Yet Time
John 7:1-13

Jesus' brothers said to him, "You ought to leave here and go to Judea, so that your disciples may see the miracles you do. No one who wants to become a public figure acts in secret. Since you are doing these things, show yourself to the world." For even his own brothers did not believe in him.

Discover Living Water

Therefore Jesus told them, "The right time for me has not yet come; for you any time is right. The world cannot hate you, but it hates me because I testify that what it does is evil. You go to the Feast. I am not yet going up to this Feast, because for me the right time has not yet come." Having said this, he stayed in Galilee.

However, after his brothers had left for the Feast, he went also, not publicly, but in secret. (John 7:3-10, NIV)

Jesus has lost the crowd that was following him, so his brothers get together in this passage to revive his campaign. They have a great idea for Jesus to win back some of his popularity.

The Feast of the Tabernacles was about to begin. It was a huge celebration in Jerusalem that lasted seven days. Jewish families would stay in tent-like shelters to symbolize how they lived in the desert before they entered the Promised Land. This yearly feast was a celebration of how God took care of them during that time.

The brothers thought Jesus should go to the Feast and do some miracles in public so people could see how great he was. They were concerned about his reputation (which obviously had an effect on theirs). They thought this strategy would do the trick. But

Jesus lets them know that the only agenda he's going to follow is the one set before him by God. And no one is going to sway him—not even his brothers.

In this passage we get the first inkling that God's timing is not our timing. At first glance this helpful suggestion from Jesus' brothers seems like a good idea. But the time is not yet right. Jesus ends up going to the Feast but not when his brothers thought he should go. There was a reason for his timing, of course, but it didn't make sense until later on. That's often how it is with God.

Drink From Living Water

A man was once trying to outsmart God, so he said, "God, is it true that a thousand years for you is like a day?" And God said, "Yes, that's true." The man said, "Then does it follow that a thousand dollars for you is like a penny?" And God said, "Well, yes." So the man said, "Then can I have a penny?" And God said, "Sure, just a second."

Jesus reveals in this passage that God's timing may not be our timing. But we can trust that because it is God's, it is always right. Even if it takes a second to see it.

① Do you think Jesus' brothers wanted Jesus to go to the Feast out of concern for him or themselves? Why?

② Have you ever asked God for something and had it come at a different time than you wanted? If so, was the timing better or worse?

③ In what area of your life do you need to trust God's timing?

Sometimes when we look back on the way God has worked, it helps us trust God more with our future. What are some things you can remember that God has done in your life?

Right Judgment
John 7:14-31

"Has not Moses given you the law? Yet not one of you keeps the law. Why are you trying to kill me?"

"You are demon-possessed," the crowd answered. "Who is trying to kill you?"

Jesus said to them, "I did one miracle, and you are all astonished. Yet, because Moses gave you circumcision (though actually it did not come from Moses, but from the patriarchs), you circumcise a child on the Sabbath. Now if a child can be circumcised on the Sabbath so that the law of Moses may not be broken, why are you angry with me for healing the whole man on the Sabbath? Stop judging by mere appearances, and make a right judgment." (John 7:19-24, NIV)

Discover Living Water

One of the characteristics of a really good movie is a surprise ending—when you find out the bad guy was really the good guy, and the good guy was really the bad guy! Immediately you go back in your head to remember the things each of them did, and you realize you had clues all along but were totally tricked at the time.

That switch is a little like what happens in this passage. In verse 15, the Jews are initially open to Jesus, and they appear to be the good guys. In verse 19, Jesus seems unreasonably upset and paranoid, which causes him to appear to be the bad guy. A closer look reveals the truth.

The appearance of this encounter is deceiving until you understand what's going on. Jesus points out that the Jews condemned him for healing the man on the Sabbath, yet they allowed circumcision to be done on the Sabbath. This inconsistency shows how hypocritical they were. They were willing to accept circumcision but not healing. By pointing out this discrepancy, Jesus shows that they were really just looking for ways to condemn him.

Drink From Living Water

When we take a closer look at Jesus' arguments, we see he is not as unreasonable as he seems. He has a reason for his frustrations. Now things are starting to look a little different.

Often we judge a situation too soon rather than taking the time to see how it really is. That failure was the Jews' mistake too. Jesus didn't fit into their box, so they closed their ears to his truth. They were blinded from seeing who he really was, because he wasn't what they wanted him to be. Eventually, they tried to get rid of him.

Good movies with a twist show how easily we can misjudge a situation. But there are no consequences in a movie. Misjudging a situation in real life can be dangerous. When Jesus says, "Stop judging by mere appearances, and make a right judgment" (verse 24), it's a warning we should heed. And it comes from the good guy. Trust me.

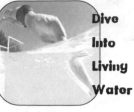

Dive Into Living Water

① Have you ever misjudged a person and thought he or she was different than he or she really was? What did that experience teach you?

② How does Jesus appear to be in this passage?

If you had been listening to Jesus, what would your impression have been?

③ In what way is Jesus misunderstood today?

Do you feel like you have an accurate understanding of who he is? Why or why not?

Living Water
John 7:32-39

On the last day of the festival, the great day, while Jesus was standing there, he cried out, "Let anyone who is thirsty come to me, and let the one who believes in me drink. As the scripture has said, 'Out of the believer's heart shall flow rivers of living water.'" Now he said this about the Spirit, which believers in him were to receive. (John 7:37-39, NRSV)

Discover Living Water

The dialogue that opens this passage indicates that Jesus was beginning to cause a stir with some of the things he was saying. Only a few had heard him; he had yet to address the crowd.

Though Jesus arrived midway through the Feast of the Tabernacles, he waited until the last day before he gave his speech. He stood and said in a loud voice, "Let anyone who is thirsty come to me, and let the one who believes in me drink" (verse 38). At first glance, you might question the timing of his teaching. The Jews had been eating and drinking for seven days. Why didn't he stand up at the beginning before they had their fill?

Of course, Jesus' timing was perfect. Because it's only after we've filled ourselves up with everything we can that we feel that deep longing. It's a longing we can't really explain.

It's kind of like that feeling you get after you open the last present at Christmas. You've looked forward to it for weeks. Now you're left feeling a little sad. It's not that you didn't have a great time. But the presents, food, and celebration didn't quite satisfy you the way you thought they would, and you feel a little empty. Jesus knew about that feeling when he stood up to teach in this passage.

Some of us attempt to fill that emptiness in unhealthy ways. We take something or drink something to make the high

Drink From Living Water

last. Sooner or later the high ends, and we are still left feeling empty.

We may try to fill the emptiness with relationships. We meet someone who seems to be the answer to our dreams. But the feeling doesn't last, so we move on. We keep going from person to person until finally we realize we are trying to fill something that a person just can't fill (just like the woman at the well). So Jesus asks, "Is anyone still thirsty?"

If we're lucky we say yes, because he knows we have a deep thirst we can't quench ourselves. We need living water, the Spirit of God, to quench it. Only one person can give this water to us.

He's the same one who stood up at the Feast of Tabernacles on the seventh day and said, "Let anyone who is thirsty come to me, and let the one who believes in me drink" (verses 37-38). The invitation still stands.

① Have you ever felt a deep longing for something? If so, when? What did you do (if anything) to try to satisfy it?

Dive Into Living Water

② What does Jesus say happens to people who drink his living water?

Have you ever experienced this?

③ In what ways can you "draw from the well" and drink the living water Christ has for you? (Think about the things you've done that have made you feel close to God and how you can do some of those things this week.)

Who Is This Man?
John 7:40–53

On hearing his words, some of the people said, "Surely this man is the Prophet."

Others said, "He is the Christ."

Still others asked, "How can the Christ come from Galilee? ..."

Thus the people were divided because of Jesus. ...

Finally the temple guards went back to the chief priests and Pharisees, who asked them, "Why didn't you bring him in?"

"No one ever spoke the way this man does," the guards declared.

"You mean he has deceived you also?" the Pharisees retorted. (John 7:40-41, 43, 45-47, NIV)

Discover Living Water

The mixed reactions that follow Jesus' speech show he caused quite a controversy by the things he said. The same is true today.

As a teacher, Christ would have been warmly received. His words were powerful and knowledgeable, and the Jews were initially impressed. However, Jesus repeatedly takes a turn in his teaching to show he is more than just a teacher. This is what makes him so controversial.

After the feeding of the five thousand, Jesus is very popular as a bread giver. Then he makes a speech about being the Bread, and the people walk away. In this passage, Jesus has declared himself the source of living water. This action is another clear step beyond teaching. Again and again, we hear Jesus make claims that show he is more than a teacher or a prophet. And he both draws and alienates people with his claims.

Here we have an issue of control. If Jesus is simply a teacher, we can sift through his words and decide whether or not we will apply them. If he is Lord, his words have the authority to sift through us and show how we *need* to apply them. The bottom line is if Jesus is just a teacher, we get to control him; if he is Lord, he controls us. But if we listen closely to his words, we realize we really don't have this choice.

Drink From Living Water

C.S. Lewis emphasizes this in *Mere Christianity* when he says, "A man who was merely a man and said the sort of things Jesus said would not be a great moral teacher. He would either be a lunatic—on a level with a man who says he is a poached egg—or else he would be the Devil of Hell. You must make your choice. Either this man was, and is, the Son of God; or else a madman or something worse. You can shut Him up for a fool, you can spit at Him and kill Him as a demon; or you can fall at His feet and call Him Lord and God. But let us not come with any patronizing nonsense about His being a great human teacher. He has not left that open to us. He did not intend to."[1]

Enough said.

Dive Into Living Water

① What was the people's reaction to Jesus after he gave his speech at the Feast (verses 40-44)?

How do you think you would have reacted?

② How do you see evidence of Nicodemus' growing faith in this passage?

What did the Jews say to him?

③ What would you say if someone asked you if Jesus was a great teacher?

What verses would you show them to discover who Jesus really is?

[1]MERE CHRISTIANITY by C.S. Lewis copyright © C.S. Lewis Pte. Ltd. 1942, 1943, 1944, 1952.

Pointing the Finger
John 8:1-11

The scribes and the Pharisees brought a woman who had been caught in adultery; and making her stand before all of them, they said to him, "Teacher, this woman was caught in the very act of committing adultery. Now in the law Moses commanded us to stone such women. Now what do you say?" They said this to test him, so that they might have some charge to bring against him. Jesus bent down and wrote with his finger on the ground. When they kept on questioning him, he straightened up and said to them, "Let anyone among you who is without sin be the first to throw a stone at her." (John 8:3-7, NRSV)

Discover Living Water

Imagine the scene. You are seated in the Temple with a group of people listening to Jesus. Suddenly the Pharisees storm in, dragging a scantily clothed woman to the front of the group. She is clearly humiliated, crying softly to herself as the Pharisees shove her in front of Jesus. They announce, "This woman was caught in the very act of committing adultery." The crowd around you gasps. You wonder why she is brought in alone. Doesn't adultery involve two?

The announcement of the Law is given: "Moses commanded us to stone such women" (verse 5). They look at Jesus. "Now what do you say?" (verse 5). You hold your breath, wondering how he is going to handle this situation. Your eyes are on the woman.

Suddenly Jesus bends down and begins to write. You shift your gaze to him. You try to strain your eyes, but you can't see what he is writing. You look around and notice everyone's eyes are on Jesus—even the woman's. Finally Jesus gets up and says, "Let anyone among you who is without sin be the first to throw a stone at her" (verse 7). Then he bends down again.

Drink From Living Water

You are no longer looking at Jesus. Now you're looking at yourself. You are thinking about all the things you've done that make it impossible to cast that stone. You feel the sting of remorse as you relive sinful thoughts and actions you carefully locked away. Suddenly you feel empathy for the woman. The only difference between you and her is the fact that she got caught.

Your thoughts are interrupted as people around you turn and walk away. You join them. As you walk outside the Temple court, you hear Jesus speak to the woman, "Has no one condemned you?" (verse 10). You turn to see what she'll say. She looks up at him and replies, "No one, sir" (verse 11). Your eyes are riveted on Jesus. He says, "Neither do I condemn you" (verse 11). You feel a sweet sense of relief. As you turn to walk away, you hear Jesus' final words: "Go your way, and from now on do not sin again" (verse 11).

Those words echo in your heart as you make your way toward home. You know they aren't just for the woman. They are for you too.

Dive Into Living Water

① Why do you think Jesus bent down to write when the woman was brought before him?

What do you think he was trying to do?

② What does this story tell you about Jesus' attitude toward sin?

③ If you were brought before Jesus, for what sin would you have been caught?

How can you obey Jesus' words to "Go your way, and from now on do not sin again" (verse 11)?

Light of the World
John 8:12-30

When Jesus spoke again to the people, he said, "I am the light of the world. Whoever follows me will never walk in darkness, but will have the light of life."

The Pharisees challenged him, "Here you are, appearing as your own witness; your testimony is not valid."

Discover Living Water

Jesus answered, "Even if I testify on my own behalf, my testimony is valid, for I know where I came from and where I am going. But you have no idea where I come from or where I am going. You judge by human standards; I pass judgment on no one. But if I do judge, my decisions are right, because I am not alone. I stand with the Father, who sent me."

Then they asked him, "Where is your father?"

"You do not know me or my Father," Jesus replied. "If you knew me, you would know my Father also." (John 8:12-16, 19, NIV)

Jesus has already called himself the Bread of life. In this passage, he calls himself the Light of the world. These two images represent different attributes of his character. As Bread, Jesus brings us satisfaction and fulfillment. As Light, Jesus gives us wisdom and understanding. Light is what we need to be able to discern the truth. And that's what Jesus teaches us in this passage.

At times in our lives, God's presence reveals truth we don't want to see. So we turn our backs and stay in darkness. The truth is hard to swallow when we know it's going to require us to change. Changing is what the Jews resisted in this passage. Accepting Jesus as God's Son would completely transform the theology they spent so many years following, and this was more uncomfortable for them. They couldn't accept his teaching. Yet somehow they couldn't walk away.

You would think that after getting so many answers they didn't want to hear, they would have stopped following Jesus around. But they never did.

Drink From Living Water

Something about Jesus intrigued them enough that they couldn't stop questioning him. Even though they didn't want the Light, they were drawn to it.

It reminds me of those lights that draw bugs in and zap them. After enough zaps you would think the bugs would know what was going to happen to them, but they still can't stay away. After enough zaps you would think the Pharisees would know that too. But they just keep buzzing around Jesus, getting answers they don't want to hear.

Of course, some of them do finally come into the light and put their faith in him (verse 30). They were the ones wise enough to see that following Jesus around and debating him wasn't nearly as fulfilling as simply following him.

① Why do you think the Pharisees kept following Jesus?

Dive Into Living Water

What does that tell you about how they felt about him?

② What are the qualities of light that are found in Jesus?

How have you experienced them?

③ Where are you in relation to Jesus' light? Are you walking where it's bright, dim, or dark?

What would it take for you to move where it's brighter (and be closer to him)?

Freedom and Slavery
John 8:31–47

Discover

Living

Water

To the Jews who had believed him, Jesus said, "If you hold to my teaching, you are really my disciples. Then you will know the truth, and the truth will set you free."

They answered him, "We are Abraham's descendants and have never been slaves of anyone. How can you say that we shall be set free?"

Jesus replied, "I tell you the truth, everyone who sins is a slave to sin. Now a slave has no permanent place in the family, but a son belongs to it forever. So if the Son sets you free, you will be free indeed." (John 8:31-36, NIV)

Have you ever heard a radio announcer go on and on about an incredible deal, and then in the last ten seconds of the commercial he starts talking in hyperspeed to list off the conditions? Suddenly he sounds like a munchkin on *The Wizard of Oz*, and you can't make out a word he says. That's the point. He's required to give you the conditions, but he doesn't want you to hear them. You might not buy the product.

That's what the devil is like when speaking to us about sin. The promise is alluring and loud, convincing us to do something we know we shouldn't do. The conditions are so faint we can barely hear them. If we listened, we might hear what Jesus says in this passage, "Everyone who sins is a slave to sin" (verse 34). You don't want to hear these words when you're thinking about

sinning. But if you keep giving in to the same sin, you'll eventually experience the consequences.

I once heard an alcoholic talk about when he realized he had a problem. He said he was having a blast drinking, and it was totally under control. All of a sudden the time came when he no longer wanted alcohol; he needed it. He described his revelation by saying, "It was as if there was a knock on the door, and I opened it to find a pile of booze with a note. The note said, 'We've been happy to serve you for a while. But from now on, you will serve us.'"

The thing about sin is that it never delivers the freedom it promises. Instead, it makes you

Drink

From

Living

Water

its slave. The devil doesn't want you to hear the conditions when you're making the choice to sin. That's when we need to turn up the volume on Jesus' words: "Everyone who sins is a slave to sin" (verse 34).

Jesus goes on to say there is an alternative. Freedom. It's found through life with him. "If the Son sets you free, you will be free indeed" (verse 36). No munchkin voices are attached to this promise. And the only condition is that you have to claim it.

① What does Jesus say in verse 31 about being his disciple?

Based on this verse, would you call yourself a disciple?

② Where have you seen evidence of sin leading to slavery in your own life?

Have you found yourself addicted to anything?

③ What could help you hear Jesus' voice more clearly during the times you are tempted to sin?

Do you have a friend who can help hold you accountable?

The God of the Present
John 8:48-59

"Your father Abraham rejoiced at the thought of seeing my day; he saw it and was glad."

"You are not yet fifty years old," the Jews said to him, "and you have seen Abraham!"

"I tell you the truth," Jesus answered, "before Abraham was born, I am!" At this, they picked up stones to stone him, but Jesus hid himself, slipping away from the temple grounds. (John 8:56-59, NIV)

Discover Living Water

When Jesus refers to himself as "I am," it sounds like he is using the wrong verb tense. This happened once before in the Bible. Remember Moses? He was out tending sheep when suddenly he began to have a conversation with a burning bush (Exodus 3). (The weird thing is the bush was the one that started it.) Now before you start conversing with shrubbery, let me remind you that as far as I know, this has only happened once in the course of history. It was a very big moment for Moses—because it was when he first met God.

God told Moses that he was being sent to lead the Israelites out of Egypt. Moses asked God what he should say when asked who sent him. God said, "I AM has sent me to you" (Exodus 3:14). Sound familiar?

When Jesus used the words, *I am*, to describe himself, the Jews knew he was claiming to be God. That's why they got so upset. Jesus was saying that the same God who met Moses was now conversing with them. And this is the same God who meets us today.

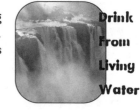

Drink From Living Water

You might be thinking, *I can't feel or see Jesus. How do I know he's there?* There is a scene from *Indiana Jones and the Last Crusade* when Indiana finds himself on a cliff needing to get to the other side of a huge cavern. The instructions on his paper say to leap—but there is nothing for him to leap on to! Finally he takes a deep breath and steps out into the nothingness. Just as he puts his weight down into the air, an invisible bridge appears. The bridge was there all the time. But Indiana didn't know it was there until he took a step of faith.

When Jesus calls himself "I am," he reminds us that although he is the God of the past, present, and future, we experience his presence in the now. Like that bridge, he is there for you when you need him. You may not be able to see him with your eyes; but if you look closely, you can experience his presence all around you. Feel him in the hug of a good friend. Hear him in the convictions of your heart. See him on the faces of the people you love. And just at that moment when you need him most, you'll find he's right there with you. All it takes to see him is a step of faith.

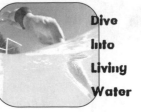

Dive Into Living Water

❶ In what ways have you experienced the presence of Jesus?

When (or where) have you seen Jesus most clearly?

When (or where) have you had trouble seeing Jesus?

❷ Have you ever taken a step of faith? If so, what happened?

❸ What step of faith might God want you to take right now?

What would it take for you to take that step?

Grace and Healing

John 9:1–15

As he went along, he saw a man blind from birth. His disciples asked him, "Rabbi, who sinned, this man or his parents, that he was born blind?"

"Neither this man nor his parents sinned," said Jesus, "but this happened so that the work of God might be displayed in his life.

Discover Living Water

As long as it is day, we must do the work of him who sent me. Night is coming, when no one can work. While I am in the world, I am the light of the world."

Having said this, he spit on the ground, made some mud with the saliva, and put it on the man's eyes. "Go," he told him, "wash in the Pool of Siloam" (this word means Sent). So the man went and washed, and came home seeing. (John 9:1-7, NIV)

Remember Job? He is the guy in the Old Testament who has a lot of really bad things happen to him. He loses his home, his children, and to top it off, he is covered with big, painful boils all over his body. Finally his wife drops by to encourage him, saying, "Curse God and die" (Job 2:9). (Not a great choice for a bride.) Just when he thinks things can't possibly get worse, his friends come by to comfort him. They tell him there must be a reason these things are happening, and it probably has to do with sin in his life. I'm sure that made him feel a lot better.

Ultimately Job learns the same lesson Jesus teaches in this passage of John—suffering is not always a consequence of sin. Job is allowed to suffer not because he was bad, but because he was good—and his suffering brought glory to God.

In the end Job receives everything back and more, but it is because of Job's willingness to suffer that God's grace is revealed.

The disciples find out from Jesus that this man's blindness— like Job's suffering—is not a result of sin. It is an avenue for God's glory. We are not given much information about how good or bad this man is, but we know his blindness caused him to suffer. Blind people had to beg in order to survive, so he not only spent his days in darkness, but he was also reduced to the dregs of society. But Jesus changes all that.

Drink From Living Water

After calling himself the Light of the world, Jesus fulfills his calling symbolically by bringing light to this man's eyes. The change is so drastic that people who knew him no longer recognized him (verse 9). After being marginalized for so many years, this man is now the center of attention, telling his story of healing. And his story leads people to find out for themselves who Christ is.

This passage reaffirms that suffering can lead to new life and a chance to witness the glory of God. Job experiences this truth when he can see from a different perspective. The blind man experiences it when he can see.

Dive Into Living Water

❶ What does Jesus teach the disciples in this passage?

How do you think their theology changed after this incident? (Theology is what you believe about God.)

❷ How did the man's neighbors and friends respond to his healing?

If you were the man, how would their responses have made you feel?

❸ Why do you think God allows suffering?

Can you see anything good that could come of it?

Has anything good happened as a result of suffering in your own life?

Eyes to See

John 9:16–41

A second time they summoned the man who had been blind. "Give glory to God," they said. "We know this man is a sinner."

He replied, "Whether he is a sinner or not, I don't know. One thing I do know. I was blind but now I see!"

Then they asked him, "What did he do to you? How did he open your eyes?"

He answered, "I have told you already and you did not listen. Why do you want to hear it again? Do you want to become his disciples, too?"

Then they hurled insults at him and said, "You are this fellow's disciple! We are disciples of Moses! We know that God spoke to Moses, but as for this fellow, we don't even know where he comes from." (John 9:24-29, NIV)

Discover Living Water

My favorite thing about science class was when we got to do experiments. To be truthful, it was the only part of science class I liked. Sometimes we got to dissect lambs' eyes and frogs' organs, which was always fun. But the most fascinating part of class was when we got to look at things under a microscope. It amazed me to see how many millions of organisms lived in a single drop of water. The microscope opened up a view of the world that we couldn't see on our own.

In this passage, Jesus demonstrates that he is like a spiritual microscope. The blind man tells people that Jesus is the reason for his newfound vision. The Pharisees discredit the man's healing, saying Jesus couldn't possibly be from God. As the blind man's vision gets clearer and clearer about who Jesus is, theirs gets foggier and foggier—because they refuse to accept his testimony. In the end, the blind man has more spiritual vision than the Pharisees.

Drink From Living Water

Jesus shows himself to be a great teacher, because he uses the blind man's healing to reveal spiritual truth. In verse 39 he says, "For judgment I have come into this world, so that the blind will see and those who see will become blind." That's exactly what happens in this chapter.

At the beginning of the chapter, the blind man is not only physically blind; he is spiritually blind too. He has no idea who Jesus is. Jesus heals him physically but also gives him new eyes to see spiritually. The man's newfound faith in Christ is revealed in verse 27 when he says to the Pharisees, "Do you want to become his disciples, too?" His question indicates that he is already a disciple himself, and he challenges the Pharisees to join him.

Unfortunately, the Pharisees feel they have all the spiritual vision they need. Their pride doesn't allow them to receive this man's testimony or be open to Jesus' help. Sadly, their narrow vision ultimately costs them their sight.

In a sense it's as if they are staring at a drop of water trying to determine what it's made of, when all the while there's a microscope waiting to show them. Jesus is that microscope. Through him, we truly see.

❶ How did the blind man's life change as a result of being healed by Jesus?

Do you think it was hard for him at all? Why or why not?

❷ How does the blind man grow in his confidence about Christ in this passage?

Have you grown in your own confidence about Christ in your life? Why or why not?

❸ Do you know anyone who is blind to Christ right now? Pray that you might have an opportunity to share your faith—and that God may give them eyes to see.

The Good Shepherd
John 10:1-21

So again Jesus said to them, "Very truly, I tell you, I am the gate for the sheep. All who came before me are thieves and bandits; but the sheep did not listen to them. I am the gate. Whoever enters by me will be saved, and will come in and go out and find pasture. The thief comes only to steal and kill and destroy. I came that they may have life, and have it abundantly.

Discover

Living

Water

"I am the good shepherd. The good shepherd lays down his life for the sheep." (John 10:7-11, NRSV)

Sheep are not the brightest of creatures. They may be cute, but they're dumb. (I'm not being mean; ask a farmer.) I had a friend who was driving through the country when she saw some sheep on the road. She slowed down to avoid running into them, and a sheep ran into her car! Thanks to heavy padding, the sheep was in better shape than her car. My friend witnessed firsthand why sheep need a little help.

Usually that help comes in the form of a shepherd. That is the image Jesus borrows in this passage. Sometimes a shepherd guides sheep gently, using his staff to direct their path. Other times he uses a firmer touch. But when sheep go too far in the wrong direction, the shepherd has to go to great lengths to get them back.

Sometimes we are like sheep. Jesus calls himself a Shepherd to let us know he can provide the direction we need. This metaphor was very familiar to Jewish listeners; most of them knew shepherding the way we know computer technology.

That's why they probably weren't confused when Jesus said he was

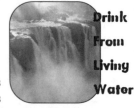

Drink

From

Living

Water

also a gate for the sheep.

At first it seems like he's mixing metaphors, but Jews knew that shepherds who wanted to protect their sheep would sleep at the entrance of the sheep pen to make sure none of them were stolen during the night. In a sense they would "become the gate" to ensure the safety of their sheep. Jesus borrows this image to let us know he is the entrance to the sheep pen—and the

Shepherd who protects us when we come in.

In this passage, Jesus alludes to the Crucifixion when he says, "I lay down my life for the sheep" (verse 15). The people who heard him couldn't have known that's exactly what he would do. But that's not where the story would end.

Jesus alludes to the Resurrection when he says he will lay down his life "in order to take it up again" (verse 17). These were strange words, and some of the Jews thought he was demon possessed. But others knew these were not the words of a man possessed by a demon.

They were the words of a man possessed by God.

❶ How is Jesus like a shepherd?

Dive Into Living Water

What does he say in this passage about the way he shepherds us?

❷ How have you been like a sheep?

Have you ever wandered away from God and experienced God's finding you?

❸ If you were to describe your place as a sheep in God's flock, where would you be right now? following closely and obediently? in the back of the flock barely tagging on? or away from the flock altogether?

One With the Father
John 10:22-42

The Jews gathered around him, saying, "How long will you keep us in suspense? If you are the Christ, tell us plainly."
Jesus answered, "I did tell you, but you do not believe. The miracles I do in my Father's name speak for me, but you do not believe because you are not my sheep. My sheep listen to my voice; I know them, and they follow me. I give them eternal life, and they shall never perish; no one can snatch them out of my hand. My Father, who has given them to me, is greater than all; no one can snatch them out of my Father's hand. I and the Father are one." Again the Jews picked up stones to stone him. (John 10:24-31, NIV)

Discover Living Water

This scene reminds me of a good courtroom drama. Jesus is on the stand. The Jews gather around him forming a jury. They want to know once and for all who he really is. The prosecutor steps to the front of the group and says, "How long will you keep us in suspense? If you are the Christ, tell us plainly" (verse 24). They wait for his response. But Jesus knows his response is not the one they want to hear. If it were, they would have heard it already.

When we look back over the last ten chapters, we can see that Jesus has been speaking of his identity all along. When he said he was the Bread of life, he demonstrated that he could provide for their needs. When he said he was Living Water, he communicated he had the ability to give them new life. When he said he was the Light

of the world, he revealed he could show them the truth. But if anyone still had questions about Jesus' identity, they are settled in this passage.

When the Jews ask Jesus to tell them plainly if he is the Christ, he says, "I and the Father are one" (verse 30). In this statement, Jesus makes a clear confession that he sees himself equal to God. Now the Jews are forced to respond to his claims.

Drink From Living Water

They had told him they wanted to hear plainly if he was the Christ. But their response shows what they wanted to hear was that he wasn't the Christ. Like a prosecutor baiting a witness, the Jews obviously had an agenda for what they wanted Jesus to say. When he didn't give the response they were looking for, they wanted to stone him. But he was able to escape their grasp.

As the Good Shepherd, he will eventually lay down his life for his sheep. For now the people have to decide whether or not they want to be his sheep. His testimony has been heard. Now it's time for the jury to decide.

① Why do the Jews ask Jesus if he is the Christ?

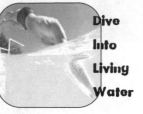

Did they really want to know? Do you know anyone like that?

② What does Jesus say in verse 27 about how we can identify his sheep?

What does he say about his sheep in verse 28?

How does this make you feel?

③ Do you know anyone who needs to read verse 30 to understand who Jesus is?

How could you use that verse to be a witness to someone this week?

God's Timing
John 11:1-22

Now a man named Lazarus was sick. He was from Bethany, the village of Mary and her sister Martha. ... So the sisters sent word to Jesus, "Lord, the one you love is sick." When he heard this, Jesus said, "This sickness will not end in death. No, it is for God's glory so that God's Son may be glorified through it." Jesus loved Martha and her sister and Lazarus. Yet when he heard that Lazarus was sick, he stayed where he was two more days. ...

Discover Living Water

On his arrival, Jesus found that Lazarus had already been in the tomb for four days. Bethany was less than two miles from Jerusalem, and many Jews had come to Martha and Mary to comfort them in the loss of their brother. When Martha heard that Jesus was coming, she went out to meet him, but Mary stayed at home.

"Lord," Martha said to Jesus, "if you had been here, my brother would not have died. But I know that even now God will give you whatever you ask." (John 11:1, 3-6, 17-22, NIV)

At first glance, Jesus does something in this passage that doesn't appear to make sense. Mary and Martha have made a special effort to get word to him that Lazarus is sick. It's clear Jesus cares about these people very much, because his love for them is mentioned several times. Yet verse 6 says, "When he heard that Lazarus was sick, he stayed where he was two more days."

After Jesus' love for Lazarus is proclaimed in verse 5, it seems like verse 6 should say, "When he heard Lazarus was sick, he ran to his house to heal him." But it doesn't say that. Jesus' response doesn't seem to make sense until we watch how the story unfolds.

So often with God's timing, we don't understand what is happening until we view it in retrospect. Then we have the whole picture, which is what God sees all along. Imagine how Mary and Martha felt when they heard that Jesus decided to stay where he was. They must have wondered if Jesus cared. Aren't we like that too?

Drink From Living Water

When we pray for something we desperately want and nothing happens, it's easy to wonder if God cares. At that point we have to realize that God is at work, even if we can't see it. In hindsight we will understand the reasons that things happened as they did, even though they appeared to make no sense at the time.

When Martha comes to meet Jesus after Lazarus has died, she expresses what we feel when we think God is too late.

"Lord, if you had been here, my brother would not have died" (verse 21). What Martha could not have seen then was that Jesus was waiting for Lazarus to die to demonstrate the miracle of resurrection. Mary and Martha just wanted their brother healed; Jesus wanted more. Sometimes that's the way it is with us.

This passage reveals that our plans for God pale in comparison to the plans God has for us. And because of that, we have to trust. Sometimes our plans have to die so that God's plans can begin. That is when true miracles happen.

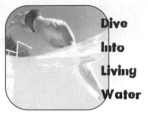

Dive Into Living Water

① What does Jesus say about Lazarus' sickness in verse 4?

Were Mary and Martha there to hear it? How does this story help you understand what you might not know about the way God is at work in your life?

② Does Jesus appear to care for Mary, Martha, and Lazarus in this passage? Why or why not?

③ With what prayer request do you need to trust God's timing?

How does this passage help you do that?

Back From the Dead
John 11:23–57

Jesus said to her, "Your brother will rise again." Martha said to him, "I know that he will rise again in the resurrection on the last day." Jesus said to her, "I am the resurrection and the life. Those who believe in me, even though they die, will live, and everyone who lives and believes in me will never die. Do you believe this?" She said to him, "Yes, Lord, I believe that you are the Messiah, the Son of God, the one coming into the world. ..."

Discover Living Water

Jesus said, "Take away the stone." Martha, the sister of the dead man, said to him, "Lord, already there is a stench because he has been dead four days." Jesus said to her, "Did I not tell you that if you believed, you would see the glory of God?" (John 11:23-27, 39-40, NRSV)

Although Jesus has done miracles up to this point, nothing surpasses the miracle he does in this passage. When Jesus arrives in Bethany, Lazarus is no longer sick—he's dead. The mourning has begun. It is too late for a healing, but it is not too late for a resurrection. Amazingly, that is what Jesus is about to do.

When Jesus says to Martha, "Your brother will rise again" (verse 23), Martha believes it; but she thinks he is referring to the afterlife. Once again we see how God's timing differs from ours. Only this time God's timing is sooner. When Jesus says, "I am the resurrection and the life" (verse 25), Martha trusts Jesus, even though she cannot possibly imagine what he has in mind to do. We see her faith in verse 27, though she is undoubtedly disappointed and saddened by her brother's death.

One of the great discoveries we make about Jesus in this passage is how he comes alongside us when we are sad. Even though he knows that Lazarus will come back to life, he cries with **Drink From Living Water** Mary and Martha. Soon their mourning will turn to dancing—but they're not dancing yet.

Finally the moment arrives, and Jesus tells them to remove the stone from the tomb. Martha feels it's her duty to remind Jesus that Lazarus has been there awhile, and it's gonna stink (that's the direct Greek translation). However, just as Martha trusted Jesus when he didn't do what she wanted, now she has to trust him doing what she doesn't want. Soon she will see why. The stone is removed and Jesus amazes the crowd with his words, "Lazarus, come out" (verse 43)! Even more amazing is what happens next: He does.

This event creates quite a stir. People who witness it see that Jesus is much more than a teacher. He is able to give new life. Many people put their faith in him, and this worries the chief priests and Pharisees. They know Jesus must be stopped.

However, the resurrection of Lazarus shows that Jesus can't be stopped, even in death. Lazarus' earthly resurrection is a sign of the resurrection power Jesus holds in his hands.

While Lazarus will eventually die again, the next time Lazarus rises, it will be for good.

❶ Why do you think Jesus cries with Mary and Martha when he knows what he is about to do?

**Dive
Into
Living
Water**

What does that tell you about Jesus?

❷ How does Martha show her faith in Jesus in this passage?

How can her faith be an example to us?

❸ Where do you need to experience Christ's resurrection power in your life?

How does this passage encourage you?

Scandalous Love
John 12:1-11

Mary took a pound of costly perfume made of pure nard, anointed Jesus' feet, and wiped them with her hair. The house was filled with the fragrance of the perfume. But Judas Iscariot, one of his disciples (the one who was about to betray him), said, "Why was this perfume not sold for three hundred denarii and the money given to the poor?" (He said this not because he cared about the poor, but because he was a thief; he kept the common purse and used to steal what was put into it.) Jesus said, "Leave her alone. She bought it so that she might keep it for the day of my burial. You always have the poor with you, but you do not always have me." (John 12:3-8, NRSV)

Discover Living Water

When I was in Paris, one of my favorite sights was the Notre Dame Cathedral. The architecture of the building is spectacular, but when you look closely at the walls and columns, you see that all the paintings, sculptures, and drawings bear witness to Jesus Christ.

Notre Dame was constructed during the French Revolution. While thousands of people didn't have food to eat, thousands of dollars were poured into erecting this great cathedral. I can only imagine the thoughts of the people during that time, looking at starvation and poverty all around them while this extravagant building was being constructed. Yet hundreds of years later, it stands as a beautiful testimony to Jesus Christ.

In this passage, Mary is chastised for honoring Jesus in an extravagant way. She takes expensive perfume, worth about twelve thousand dollars by today's standards, and pours it on Jesus' feet. It was an act of worship that could have been seen as wasteful and unnecessary. Judas says what others were probably thinking when he asks, "Why was this perfume not sold for three hundred denarii and the money given to the poor?" (verse 5). Even though his motives were wrong, his words carried a ring of truth. Yet Jesus, friend of the poor, dismisses Judas' words and commends Mary's act of worship. Why?

Drink From Living Water

Jesus knows that people need to worship as much as they need to be fed. Even in the poorest places, people express this need through art, dance, and song. People have needs that are more than physical; they are emotional and spiritual beings too. Mary brings these parts of herself to Jesus in this humble and costly gesture.

Perfume was associated not only with festivity but also with burials. Mary's action is a sign that Jesus is on his way to the cross. Jesus accepts Mary's anointing as an act of symbolism and sacrifice, and he honors her for it. Her act illustrates our need and God's desire for creative expressions of worship.

Notre Dame might have been an extravagant act of worship during a time in history when resources were deficient. But imagine the spiritual deficiency we would have if the cathedral had never been built.

① Why do you think this story is recorded in the Bible?

Dive
Into
Living
Water

What does it show us about worship?

② Look at Jesus' words in verse 8. Why do you think he says that?

What do you think he means?

③ Where have you witnessed extravagant acts of worship?

Do you feel they glorify God? Why or why not?

The Audience of One
John 12:12-26

Jesus found a young donkey and sat on it; as it is written: "Do not be afraid, daughter of Zion. Look, your king is coming, sitting on a donkey's colt!" His disciples did not understand these things at first; but when Jesus was glorified, then they remembered that these things had been written of him and had been done to him. ...

Discover Living Water

The Pharisees then said to one another, "You see, you can do nothing. Look, the world has gone after him! ..."

Jesus answered them, "The hour has come for the Son of Man to be glorified. Very truly, I tell you, unless a grain of wheat falls into the earth and dies, it remains just a single grain; but if it dies, it bears much fruit." (John 12:14-16, 19, 23-24, NRSV)

I used to work with a youth pastor who had pictures of students all over his walls. Right in the middle of all his pictures was a large sticker that I will never forget. It said in big letters: "Now serving an audience of one."

That's what Jesus is doing in this passage. For a brief moment, he's receiving praise from the people. They worship him and proclaim him King. The words of Zechariah 9:9 are being fulfilled. (Look it up if you have your Bible). The Pharisees realize something big is happening, and their reaction in verse 19 indicates they are not pleased. They can tell that people are ready to put Jesus on a throne.

But Jesus is getting ready to be put on a cross instead. How tempting it must have been for him to stay and be worshiped instead of going on to be crucified. But Jesus never lost sight of his mission. He was serving an audience of one. That led him to fulfill his destiny.

In verse 24, Jesus gives a great parable for what he's about to do. He uses the image of a seed to describe his **Drink From Living Water** death. When a kernel of wheat is buried, it springs forth from the ground, producing grain that contains more seeds. Those seeds are planted, and more seeds are produced. Soon a single seed is responsible for covering an entire field of wheat. That is a great analogy for what's going to happen to Jesus' ministry.

If he had stayed King of the Jews, he would have stopped short of being King of the world.

And that's the King he came to be. Though he's honored for a moment in this passage, the acclaim pales in comparison to the way he will be honored after the cross. But Jesus has to die to make this happen.

In verse 23 Jesus says, "The hour has come for the Son of Man to be glorified." The next several chapters suggest the opposite is true. Glory to God doesn't always appear glorious. Yet in the end, it's the only glory that prevails.

Now serving an audience of one—those are good words to live by. And in Jesus' case, they're good words to die by too.

❶ How did the disciples view what was happening in this passage?

Dive Into Living Water

How do you think they felt while it was happening?

❷ What did the Pharisees say when Jesus was being honored (verse 19)? Do you think their comment was an overstatement?

What does their response show you about how threatened they felt?

❸ How does this passage show that Jesus is fulfilling Old Testament prophecy about the Messiah?

Does this bring confidence to your faith? How can this help you in your witness to others?

The Time to Decide
John 12:27-50

Jesus said to them, "The light is with you for a little longer. Walk while you have the light, so that the darkness may not overtake you. If you walk in the darkness, you do not know where you are going. While you have the light, believe in the light, so that you may become children of light." After Jesus had said this, he departed and hid from them. ... Then Jesus cried aloud: "Whoever believes in me believes not in me but in him who sent me. ... I do not judge anyone who hears my words and does not keep them, for I came not to judge the world, but to save the world. (John 12:35-36, 44, 47, NRSV)

Discover Living Water

In this passage, Jesus gives the crowd one last chance to consider his claims. In verse 35 he expresses the urgency of the moment when he says, "The light is with you for a little longer. Walk while you have the light, so that the darkness may not overtake you."

This same decision faces us today. And in a way it's just as urgent. We don't know when our lives will end, but at that time there will be no more decision making. We will have already made our choice. And we will spend the rest of eternity in light or darkness.

But while we are here, the light is available to us if we want it. All we have to do is believe in Jesus Christ. Only those who choose not to believe will end up in darkness. That's not God's choice for us. It's a choice we make for ourselves.

After all the miraculous signs Jesus has done, some people still do not believe in him. The same is true today. The evidence is all around us that God exists. We see it in creation with the unfolding of each new day. We see it in the love we receive from others.

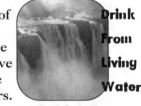

Drink From Living Water

We see it in people who make sacrifices to help those in need. We see it in the very presence of God who visited this planet in the person of Jesus Christ.

Jesus says that when people believe in him, they believe in the one who sent him (verse 44). This is what leads to eternal life. God offers us the chance to believe by sending us God's Son—but we must respond for the relationship to begin. And Jesus gives us the invitation in this passage.

We may wonder why God came in such a quiet way. It's so we would have the freedom to choose. God sent Jesus to give us a glimpse of eternity. Someday Jesus will come again, and we'll have more than a glimpse—we will see him as the King he is. And at that time there will be nothing left to choose.

Dive Into Living Water

❶ What does Jesus mean when he says, "believe in the light" (verse 36)? How do we do this?

❷ What does verse 35 say about people who walk in darkness? Do you know anyone who is walking in darkness right now?

❸ Think of three friends who need to be brought into the light. What could you do this month to introduce them to Jesus?

Servant Leadership
John 13:1–17

Jesus knew that the Father had put all things under his power, and that he had come from God and was returning to God; so he got up from the meal, took off his outer clothing, and wrapped a towel around his waist. After that, he poured water into a basin and began to wash his disciples' feet, drying them with the towel that was wrapped around him. He came to Simon Peter, who said to him, "Lord, are you going to wash my feet?" Jesus replied, "You do not realize now what I am doing, but later you will understand." "No," said Peter, "you shall never wash my feet." Jesus answered, "Unless I wash you, you have no part with me." "Then, Lord," Simon Peter replied, "not just my feet but my hands and my head as well!" (John 13:3-9, NIV)

Discover Living Water

If you were asked which story best describes what it means to be a Christian, this is it. Jesus knows he is about to go to the Father. He is with his disciples for the very last time. Now he wants to show them his power in a way they will never forget. He does it by washing their feet.

I'm sure the disciples were shocked. They were still riding high on the praise Jesus received on Palm Sunday. (I can just see them waving to the crowd saying, "I'm with *him*!") Their leader was finally getting the attention he deserved. He was worshiped and adored. But Jesus wanted his disciples to see a different kind of power, the kind he was about to reveal on the cross.

In this world we've come to see power as the ability to dine in fancy restaurants, to dress in elegant clothes, and to drive expensive cars. What if you knew someone could do all those things but chose not to? Wouldn't the choice make that person even more powerful?

Verse 3 says, "Jesus knew that the Father had put all things under his power." You would think the next verse would say, "So he told his disciples to worship him." Instead Jesus wraps a towel around his waist and washes the grime off their feet.

Drink From Living Water

You can almost hear the horror in Peter's voice in verse 6 when he says, "Lord, are you going to wash my feet?" (They were probably pretty gross.) However, Jesus tells Peter that unless he washes his feet, Peter has no part in him. The disciples learn that foot washing is part of discipleship.

Today, there are many ways of washing people's feet. For $25 to $30 a month, organizations like Compassion International, World Vision, and ChildReach make it possible for you to feed, clothe, and educate a Third-World child. That's a dollar a day or less. By giving up your spending money and putting it toward sponsoring a child, you would be "washing that child's feet."

This idea is just one example of foot washing; there are many others. The question is, Will you do it at all? Jesus says, "I have set you an example that you should do as I have done for you" (verse 15). We are left to translate his words into action.

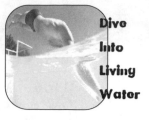

Dive Into Living Water

① What does verse 1 say about what Jesus was about to do with his disciples?

What does that tell you about the way Jesus loves?

② Have you ever had your feet washed? How did it feel?

How do you think the disciples felt while Jesus was doing this for them?

③ How can you "wash someone's feet" this week?

Pray about sponsoring a child or making some other kind of sacrifice to show Christ's love in a tangible way.

Tests of Loyalty
John 13:18-38

After he had said this, Jesus was troubled in spirit and testified, "I tell you the truth, one of you is going to betray me."... "It is the one to whom I will give this piece of bread when I have dipped it in the dish." Then, dipping the piece of bread, he gave it to Judas Iscariot, son of Simon.... My children, I will be with you only a little longer. You will look for me, and just as I told the Jews, so I tell you now: Where I am going, you cannot come.... Simon Peter asked him, "Lord, where are you going?" Jesus replied, "Where I am going, you cannot follow now, but you will follow later." Peter asked, "Lord, why can't I follow you now? I will lay down my life for you." Then Jesus answered, "Will you really lay down your life for me? I tell you the truth, before the rooster crows, you will disown me three times!" (John 13:21, 26, 33, 36-38, NIV)

Discover Living Water

Two betrayals are predicted in this passage. The difference is in how they play out. When Jesus predicts these betrayals, he lets the disciples (and the rest of us) know that we are weak, but he is strong. Our faith must rely on his strength rather than our own.

After Jesus predicts Judas' betrayal, Judas leaves. He will never come back. After Judas leaves, Jesus announces to the disciples that he is going somewhere they cannot go. After following him so long, they were probably saddened by his words.

Ultimately Peter can't contain himself. (This should not surprise us because Peter can never contain himself.) In verse 37, he blurts out, "Lord, why can't I follow you?" Then, as if he's delivering a line in a movie,

he says dramatically, "I will lay down my life for you." I can just imagine how pleased Peter was with himself after this brave statement of loyalty. But his pride is shattered when Jesus counters him with the truth: "Before the rooster crows, you will disown me three times!" (verse 38).

Drink From Living Water

I wonder if the other disciples were tempted to snicker at that point. Talk about being put in his place! What looked like a putdown was actually a gift to Peter in the long run. Peter would remember these words later and realize that Jesus still loved him. That's what would help him come back.

Jesus' love doesn't depend on our faithfulness to him. It depends on his faithfulness to us. When we blow it, all we have to do is come back.

That was Judas' mistake: He never did come back. Jesus didn't love him less than Peter; but Judas didn't allow himself to be loved. Accepting Jesus' love is the foundation for becoming a disciple. Both Judas and Peter would deny Jesus, but only Peter would be restored; not because Jesus rejected Judas, but because Judas rejected Jesus' love.

"The wages of sin is death, but the gift of God is eternal life in Christ Jesus" (Romans 6:23). We cannot bear our own sin, but Jesus can. Peter learns this lesson when he does the very thing he said he would never do. Unfortunately, Judas does not. Jesus' grace is always available.

We only have to accept it.

Dive Into Living Water

❶ Was there any difference between the predictions of Judas' betrayal and of Peter's denial?

What clues do we have that the two stories will end differently?

❷ What does this passage tell us about our faith?

❸ How does this passage make you feel about your relationship with Christ?

One Way to God
John 14:1–14

Thomas said to him, "Lord, we don't know where you are going, so how can we know the way?" Jesus answered, "I am the way and the truth and the life. No one comes to the Father except through me. If you really knew me, you would know my Father as well. From now on, you do know him and have seen him." (John 14:5-7, NIV)

Discover Living Water

I n *The Chronicles of Narnia* by C. S. Lewis, Aslan is the great lion that symbolizes Jesus Christ. In "The Silver Chair," Lewis tells the story of how Jill, one of the children who visits Narnia, encounters Aslan for the first time. She is desperately thirsty and finds herself standing in front of a gigantic stream. The only problem is that Aslan is in front of it. Aslan is a huge lion, so Jill is frozen in her tracks. She wants the water, but she's afraid to come close to Aslan. She doesn't know what he will do.

Finally she is so scared to move forward that she decides to look for another stream. She tells Aslan, and he calmly looks at her and says: "There is no other stream."

The lesson Jill learns from Aslan is the same lesson the disciples learn from Jesus: There is no other stream. Jesus says, "I am the way and the truth and the life. No one comes to the Father except through me" (verse 6). Jesus leaves no room for other faiths. In today's day and age, this kind of exclusivity is not popular; people would rather believe there

Drink From Living Water

are many ways to God. But Jesus says he is the only way, and our only choice is to reject or accept his claims.

Jesus' death and resurrection provide the only avenue for us to be able to know God. Romans 3:23 says that everyone has sinned and fallen short of the glory of God, and that they are justified through the redemption that comes from Jesus Christ. Jesus paved the way for us to know a holy God because he died for our sins. Through his death, our sins are forgiven. That's why Aslan tells Jill there is no other stream. Jesus Christ is the only way to get to God.

The disciples are confused in this passage because they want to go with Jesus where he is going. Jesus explains that they need to go through him instead. He will have to die to make that possible. That's why he must go before them.

Naturally they don't fully comprehend what he is talking about—but they will. After Jesus' death and resurrection, they'll understand his words through his actions. No other religion has a leader who left an empty grave. That's why there is no other stream.

❶ What does Jesus say in verse 6 about the way to God?

Dive Into Living Water

How do we find the way?

❷ How does Jesus describe the Father to his disciples in verse 9?

What does that tell you about Jesus?

❸ What does verse 2 tell you about what awaits us when we die?

When you think of heaven, how do you picture it?

Does this verse change your picture?

Comforter and Counselor
John 14:15-31

"If you love me, you will keep my commandments. And I will ask the Father, and he will give you another Advocate, to be with you forever. This is the Spirit of truth, whom the world cannot receive, because it neither sees him nor knows him. You know him, because he abides with you, and he will be in you. ..."

Discover Living Water

Jesus answered him, "Those who love me will keep my word, and my Father will love them, and we will come to them and make our home with them. ..."

"I have said these things to you while I am still with you. But the Advocate, the Holy Spirit, whom the Father will send in my name, will teach you everything, and remind you of all that I have said to you." (John 14:15-17, 23, 25-26, NRSV)

A pastor once said to me, "What you live is what you believe; everything else is just talk." That's what Christ teaches in this passage. He says, "If you love me, you will keep my commandments" (verse 15). He knows we can't do it without his help.

This help comes in the form of the Holy Spirit. Jesus says the Holy Spirit comes from the Father, just as he comes from the Father. You may wonder how God can be the Father, the Son, and the Holy Spirit and still be one God. Someone once explained it to me using water as an example. When water is heated, it becomes steam. When it's frozen, it becomes ice. But it never changes its makeup: three forms but only one substance. That's a little bit how it is with God.

The "steam" of God is the Holy Spirit. You can't see it, but you can feel its effects. Every time you help someone when you don't feel like it, there's a good chance the Holy Spirit is guiding you. (Unless it's your mom.) When you are tempted to do something wrong and a little voice is whispering not to, that's probably the Spirit too. The Spirit's role is to help you live what you believe. Christ gives us this Spirit when we come to know him.

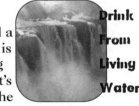

Drink From Living Water

A book called *My Heart, Christ's Home* by Bob Munger describes our hearts like little houses. When Christ makes a home in your heart, he determines what changes need to be made in order to feel at home. Sometimes a picture needs to be taken down. A television program needs to be turned off. Something might need to be taken out of the refrigerator.

Finally, Christ goes to the hall closet. That's where your deep secrets are, the things that are the hardest for you to give up. Christ knows you can't clean it yourself, so he asks you for the key. When you give him the key, he cleans it for you.

The Holy Spirit makes your heart Christ's home. That's what Christ promises in this passage. The Holy Spirit is your counselor, comforter, and friend. And even though you can't see the Spirit with your eyes, you know the Spirit is there. You feel the effects of the Spirit's presence.

The Holy Spirit helps you turn what you believe into what you live. That's what being a Christian is all about.

① According to Jesus, what is the Spirit's role in our lives?

Dive Into Living Water

What does Jesus say specifically about the Spirit in this passage?

② What evidence do you see of the Spirit in people's lives?

Who do you know who reflects the indwelling Spirit's work?

③ If your heart is a home, which room needs the most cleaning?

What can you do to make the Spirit feel more at home?

The Vine and the Branches
John 15:1-27

> *"Abide in me as I abide in you. Just as the branch cannot bear fruit by itself unless it abides in the vine, neither can you unless you abide in me. I am the vine, you are the branches. Those who abide in me and I in them bear much fruit, because apart from me you can do nothing. Whoever does not abide in me is thrown away like a branch and withers; such branches are gathered, thrown into the fire, and burned. If you abide in me, and my words abide in you, ask for whatever you wish, and it will be done for you."*
> *(John 15:4-7, NRSV)*

Discover Living Water

When I see astronauts floating through the atmosphere, I wonder what it must feel like to explore space. Of course, they are connected by cords to their rocket ship, so they can only move so far. I wonder if they are ever tempted to detach themselves from the cords and float freely through space. If they did, they'd feel the rush of being totally unbound. But not for long.

The cord, though it appears to bind them, is the very thing that gives them life. Detached from the cord, those astronauts would not be having a very good day.

In this passage, Jesus tells a parable about a vine and some branches to illustrate the same point. He is the Vine; we are the branches. Like the rocket ship cord, the Vine is our source of life. We must stay attached to the Vine to receive what we need to live.

Too often, we Christians try to do Christ's work for him. This parable teaches that we are supposed to do Christ's work *with* him. We need to be clear about our identity. Cults are formed by people who start out following God—then end up trying to be God instead. We saw this in the 1970's with Jim Jones and in the 1990's with David Koresh. The result was just what Jesus predicted in this passage.

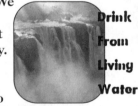

Drink From Living Water

Jesus says, "Whoever does not abide in me is thrown away like a branch and withers" (verse 6). The sad part is Jim Jones and David Koresh did not die alone. They took the lives of people who had connected themselves to a branch instead of the Vine—and in the end the choice led to death.

As Christians we must recognize where we get our life. Through Jesus we can love with supernatural power. Through Jesus we can teach great truth. Through Jesus we can experience great joy. But the secret to all these things is that they only happen through Jesus.

Jesus says, "Apart from me you can do nothing" (verse 5), and history has shown it to be true. The cult David Koresh formed was called the "Branch Davidians." What a tragedy that branch tried to make it on its own.

① Why do you think Jesus uses a vine to illustrate our relationship with him?

Dive Into Living Water

What does it tell you about how we are to live?

② What are some ways we can get disconnected from the Vine?

How can we prevent that disconnect from happening?

③ Write down some things you can do to strengthen your connection to the Vine, and make a commitment to do them this week.

Pain That Brings Joy

John 16:1–33

Discover Living Water

"I tell you the truth, you will weep and mourn while the world rejoices. You will grieve, but your grief will turn to joy. A woman giving birth to a child has pain because her time has come; but when her baby is born she forgets the anguish because of her joy that a child is born into the world. So with you: Now is your time of grief, but I will see you again and you will rejoice, and no one will take away your joy.

"I have told you these things, so that in me you may have peace. In this world you will have trouble. But take heart! I have overcome the world." (John 16:20-22, 33, NIV)

One day a friend of mine awakened to the sounds of his wife throwing up. He went to the bathroom to see if she was all right, and she lifted up her head and smiled. "Guess what?" she said excitedly. "We're pregnant!"

My friend said he felt the strangest mix of emotions. He felt terrible that his wife had to bear such pain, but he was full of joy over what that pain would become (not to mention the fact that he was born a guy).

If his wife was in pain then, it was nothing compared to how she would feel during the birth. But her pain would be forgotten the second the baby came out. That memory lapse is the phenomenon of childbirth. Jesus uses this analogy to describe what's going to happen to the disciples. When he is

taken away, they will experience pain. But their pain will not last, and their joy will be greater because of it.

We all have had similar experiences. Athletes know the more pain they endure in their workouts, the more joy they will experience

Drink From Living Water

when they compete. As a student, you know the more pain you endure in your studying, the more joy you will experience with your grades. Short-term pain produces long-term pleasure. And the pleasure is sweeter for having gone through the pain.

Jesus says that when he is taken away, the disciples will weep and mourn while the world rejoices. Although it will appear that Jesus has left them, the disciples will soon discover that pain will not have the final word.

In this world we will have trouble. Jesus says that to his disciples—but he wants us to know it too. Things happen that make us wonder if God cares. People we love die. Parents we love get divorced. Relationships we love are broken. It's easy to want to give up.

But if we endure our pain, we will discover that the trouble we have in this world is not permanent. God has a purpose in everything. The disciples will find that out. In the last verse of this passage, Jesus says that he has already overcome the world.

Now he will go on to prove it.

Dive Into Living Water

❶ When have you experienced short-term pain that led to long-term pleasure?

❷ According to Jesus, how will the disciples' experience compare to childbirth?

Why do you think he uses that analogy?

❸ When was the last time you experienced pain that eventually led to joy?

How did you feel about God at the time?

How did you feel afterward?

Jesus' Prayer
John 17:1-26

After Jesus said this, he looked toward heaven and prayed: "Father, the time has come. Glorify your Son, that your Son may glorify you. For you granted him authority over all people that he might give eternal life to all those you have given him. Now this is eternal life: that they may know you, the only true God, and Jesus

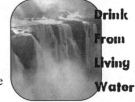

Discover
Living
Water

Christ, whom you have sent. I have brought you glory on earth by completing the work you gave me to do. And now, Father, glorify me in your presence with the glory I had with you before the world began. ...

"My prayer is not that you take them out of the world but that you protect them from the evil one. ...

"As you sent me into the world, I have sent them into the world." (John 17:1-5, 15, 18, NIV)

In this prayer, we get an inside look at Jesus' relationship with God. It is kind of like eavesdropping on a conversation between friends. Right from the start, we see that Jesus and God share in the same glory. As the prayer goes on, the intimacy of their relationship is revealed.

On the cross, Jesus will appear to be far from God's love. But here Jesus affirms that he is in the center of God's love. Here we get our first hint that God's love is not manifested in protecting us from difficulty. It is manifested in helping us overcome difficulty with God's strength. That assurance is what Jesus will experience on the cross—and he prays for that same strength in his disciples.

Why didn't Jesus pray that they be taken out of the world instead?

Imagine two fathers with their children. Each father loves his child very much. One expresses his love by protecting his child from the world. He never lets the child go outside because the child might go into the street. He doesn't teach the child to ride a bike because he is afraid the child might fall. He doesn't let the child visit friends because he is afraid of their influences.

Drink
From
Living
Water

The other father shows his love quite differently. Instead of keeping the child from the world, he equips his child for the world. He tells the child about the cars in the street so that the child learns to look both ways. He helps the child learn to withstand falls off the bike by encouraging the child to get up each time and try again. He talks to the child about influencing the child's friends instead of being influenced by them.

The love God has for us is like the love of the second father. That is what Jesus shows us in his prayer. Jesus declares that he is secure in his Father's love—even though he is headed to the cross. Ultimately, he knows God's love won't protect him from the world. But it will empower him to overcome the world.

This kind of love is what he prays for the disciples to have. It is also the love he prays for us to have. It is God's simple strategy to change the world. And Jesus' prayer is for us to accomplish it.

❶ What does Jesus model about prayer in this passage?

Dive

Into

Living

Water

How does it help us know how to pray?

❷ Underline all the things Jesus prays for his disciples. Which one stands out to you? Why?

❸ What does Jesus pray for us in this passage?

Have you experienced what he prays for? How could you be a part of Jesus' answered prayer?

Peter's Denial
John 18:1-27

Simon Peter and another disciple were following Jesus. Because this disciple was known to the high priest, he went with Jesus into the high priest's courtyard, but Peter had to wait outside at the door. The other disciple, who was known to the high priest, came back, spoke to the girl on duty there and brought Peter in. "You *are not one of his disciples, are you?" the girl at the door asked Peter. He replied, "I am not." ... As Simon Peter stood warming himself, he was asked, "You are not one of his disciples, are you?" He denied it, saying, "I am not." One of the high priest's servants, a relative of the man whose ear Peter had cut off, challenged him, "Didn't I see you with him in the olive grove?" Again Peter denied it, and at that moment a rooster began to crow. (John 18:15-17; 25-27, NIV)*

Discover Living Water

It's hard to imagine how Peter can go so quickly from ace disciple to non-disciple—until we look at ourselves. Ironically, downfalls tend to happen after the times we feel closest to God. We commit to loving our parents, sharing our faith with friends, and spending an hour reading the Bible every day. But those commitments soon become: trying not to hate our parents, saying "bless you" when friends sneeze, and opening up the Bible randomly to read, "And Saul went in to [the cave] to relieve himself" (1 Samuel 24:3). Days after saying we were going to change the world for Christ, we're wondering how to incorporate cave-peeing into our lives. This reality gives us more grace to view Peter's rapid change.

Just a few chapters earlier, Peter said to Jesus, "I will lay down my life for you" (John 13:37). Now Peter can't even admit that he knows Jesus. When Jesus is arrested and taken away, Peter and another disciple follow him. But the other disciple goes inside the court, and Peter is left standing alone. 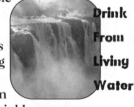 **Drink From Living Water** That's when the first denial happens.

We can learn a lesson here from Peter: Don't try to make it on your own. Sometimes we leave a camp where we're surrounded by Christians and go home to conquer the world on our own. But God has given us these Christians not only to sing songs with at camp but also to lean on when the going gets tough.

Peter learned that lesson as he stood by the fire, because he denied Christ two more times. The third time he was even questioned by someone who had seen him. Has that ever happened to you? Sometimes the people who were with us at camp are there when we blow it. And their presence makes us even more uncomfortable. It makes us realize we're compromising our love for Christ—just because we're too weak to hold on to our faith.

At that moment we need to remember Christ predicted Peter would blow it—and he still loved him. When Peter heard the cock crowing, he remembered Jesus' words—and that moment was the beginning of repentance and grace. Because even if Peter was too weak to hold on to Christ, Christ's love would not let go of Peter. That's what eventually brought him back.

❶ Why do you think Peter denied he knew Christ?

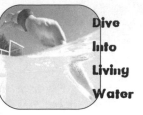

Dive

Into

Living

Water

What was he afraid of?

❷ How do you think Jesus' prediction might have helped Peter in the long run?

What did the experience show Peter about the strength of his faith?

❸ In what ways have you denied Christ?

What strengthens you to stand firm in your faith?

Pilate's Dilemma
John 18:28–40

Pilate then went back inside the palace, summoned Jesus and asked him, "Are you the king of the Jews?" "Is that your own idea," Jesus asked, "or did others talk to you about me?" "Am I a Jew?" Pilate replied. "It was your people and your chief priests who handed you over to me. What is it you have done?" Jesus said,

Discover Living Water

"My kingdom is not of this world. If it were, my servants would fight to prevent my arrest by the Jews. But now my kingdom is from another place." "You are a king, then!" said Pilate. Jesus answered, "You are right in saying I am a king. In fact, for this reason I was born, and for this I came into the world, to testify to the truth. Everyone on the side of truth listens to me." "What is truth?" Pilate asked. With this he went out again to the Jews and said, "I find no basis for a charge against him." (John 18:33-38, NIV)

There are many people who don't say no to Jesus Christ, but they never say yes either. Pontius Pilate is one of them. His story shows us that when it comes to Jesus Christ, no decision is a decision. Sometimes that's the worst kind of decision you can make.

You get the feeling when you read this passage that Pilate is being forced to do something he doesn't want to do. The Jews have brought Jesus to him because he is the Roman governor, and his decision will determine Jesus' fate. Of course, Jesus' fate is ultimately in the hands of God; but Pilate's decision will set in motion the course of events that will change history. Little did he know. Or did he?

Pilate's dialogue with the Jews indicates that he is a troubled man. He does not want to deal with Jesus. He wants the Jews to deal with him instead. But the Jews do not allow Pilate to be absolved from this decision. Pilate asks Jesus directly if he is the King of the Jews. Jesus turns the question back to him. Like everyone else, Pilate must decide for himself who Jesus is.

Drink From Living Water

Pilate doesn't affirm or deny Christ's claims. When Jesus says, "Everyone on the side of truth listens to me" (verse 37), Pilate says, "What is truth" (verse 38)? The sad irony of his question is that the truth is standing right in front of him. But Pilate is too concerned with the dilemma he faces with the Jews to consider the dilemma that will seal his destiny. Ultimately, the crowd's pressure keeps Pilate from personally affirming Christ's claims.

Today, there are many Pontius Pilates. They are the ones who know about Christianity but have avoided making a decision about personally answering Christ's claims. However, no decision is a decision by default. Christ doesn't come into our lives unless he is asked.

Pilate could never say Jesus wasn't the Christ. But because Pilate wouldn't stand up to the Jews and say Jesus was the Christ, Jesus' fate was sealed. For all time, Pilate will be remembered as the one who sentenced Christ to death.

The story of Pontius Pilate shows that when it comes to Jesus Christ, we all have to take a stand. When we don't, we may find ourselves taking one anyway.

❶ How does Pilate show that he is troubled in this passage?

Dive Into Living Water

What do his questions reveal about him?

❷ How does Jesus deal with Pilate?

Why does he wait for Pilate to tell him who he thinks he is instead of coming out and saying it?

❸ Imagine you were Pontius Pilate. How would you have handled the situation?

What would your decision have been? What about the consequences?

Sentenced Without a Crime
John 19:1–16

"Where do you come from?" [Pilate] asked Jesus, but Jesus gave him no answer. "Do you refuse to speak to me?" Pilate said. "Don't you realize I have power either to free you or to crucify you?" Jesus answered, "You would have no power over me if it were not given to you from above. Therefore the one who handed me over to you is **Discover Living Water** *guilty of a greater sin." From then on, Pilate tried to set Jesus free, but the Jews kept shouting, "If you let this man go, you are no friend of Caesar. Anyone who claims to be a king opposes Caesar. ..."*

"Shall I crucify your king?" Pilate asked. "We have no king but Caesar," the chief priests answered. Finally Pilate handed him over to them to be crucified. (John 19:9-12, 15-16, NIV)

Three times Jesus was proclaimed innocent. Then he was sentenced to death. The interrogation that began in the chapter 18 ended with Pilate's finding no basis for a charge. Yet the crowd shouted, "Crucify! Crucify!" (verse 6). Pilate shouted back, "You take him and crucify him!" (verse 6).

Nobody wanted to take responsibility for his death. They sensed something big was going to happen—and they were right. Jesus was about to die for no crime, so he could die for every crime. He was going to do this for us all.

I remember hearing a story from World War II about a priest in a concentration camp named Father Kolbe. One day he was forced to stand naked in the snow with dozens of other prisoners, while the Nazis randomly chose ten people to die. Father Kolbe was passed over; the prisoner next to him was chosen. As the man was taken away, Father Kolbe heard him say, "My poor wife, my poor children." So Father Kolbe stepped out of line. The commander came over and Father Kolbe said,

Drink From Living Water

"I would like to die in place of that man." The man was shoved back in line, and Father Kolbe took his place.

He and nine other prisoners were taken to a cell where they were given no food or water until they shriveled up and died. During their last days together, Father Kolbe led all nine prisoners to Christ. When he finally died, they found him sitting against the jail cell wall, his eyes still open. And he was smiling.

Father Kolbe had done an incredible thing by dying in another man's place. But Jesus Christ did something even greater. He died in place of us all. Romans 5:7-8 says, "Indeed, rarely will anyone die for a righteous person—though perhaps for a good person someone might actually dare to die. But God proves his love for us in that while we still were sinners Christ died for us" (NRSV). The trial in this passage is the catalyst for his death.

Pilate looks at the Jews and says, "Here is your king" (verse 14). They answer, "We have no king but Caesar" (verse 15). With that, Jesus is handed over to be crucified. There is no crime. Yet Jesus is on his way to the cross.

That won't be the end of the story. Something tells me the reason Father Kolbe was smiling when he died is that the King who preceded him was welcoming him.

① In this passage, Jesus is given the only crown he would ever wear. What was it?

What does that tell you about the kind of king that he was?

② From where does Jesus say that Pilate's power to sentence him had come?

Do you think that absolves Pilate from being responsible? Why or why not?

③ What ultimately is the reason Christ is crucified?

Did he have to die? Why or why not?

The Suffering of Christ
John 19:17-42

Carrying his own cross, he went out to the place of the Skull (which in Aramaic is called Golgotha). Here they crucified him, and with him two others—one on each side and Jesus in the middle. ...

Later, knowing that all was now completed, and so that the Scripture would be fulfilled, Jesus said, "I am thirsty." A jar of wine vinegar was there, so they soaked a sponge in it, put the sponge on a stalk of the hyssop plant, and lifted it to Jesus' lips. When he had received the drink, Jesus said, "It is finished." With that, he bowed his head and gave up his spirit. (John 19:17-18, 28-30, NIV)

Discover Living Water

When I was little, my mom used to say, "Do you know how much I love you?" I would say, "How much?" Then she would stretch out her arms as far as they would reach and say, "This much." It was kind of a silly game, but it showed me how much I was loved.

In this passage, Jesus Christ shows us how much we are loved. But he didn't just reach out his hands. He let those hands be nailed to a cross. Crucifixion was a brutal death.

First, a person was deprived of all human dignity while being stripped down, having his hands and feet nailed to a cross. In order to breathe, the victim had to push himself up with his nailed hands and feet. Eventually he became so exhausted he finally suffocated. Crucifixion was a slow, excruciating death—one of the most painful punishments ever inflicted on a human being.

The other Gospels record that as Jesus hung on the cross, people mocked him: "He saved others," they said, "but he can't save himself" (Matthew 27:42; see also Mark 15:31 and Luke 23:35). Yet precisely because he was saving others, he refrained from saving himself. How tempting it must have been to call on God to save him. Yet he humbly submitted to the sacrifice. Luke records that Jesus looked at the mockers and said, "Father, forgive them, for they do not know what they are doing" (Luke 23:34). After

Drink From Living Water

his death, some of them would be aware of what they had done.

With our sin on his shoulders, Jesus became our ultimate sacrifice. That was the great work of the cross. John 19:30 records Jesus' words: "It is finished." The work was done, and Jesus was dead.

In Mark 15:39, a centurion sees the way Jesus dies and says, "Surely this man was the Son of God." Soon more would realize that fact. But for now, as a dead man, Jesus is taken off the cross and buried. The tomb would become his temporary home.

In this passage we see the extent of Jesus Christ's love. When we ask him how much he loved us, he said, "This much." And he stretched out his arms and died.

❶ Read the passage once more to get its full impact. What stands out to you? Why?

Dive
Into
Living
Water

❷ How does Christ's suffering affect your relationship with him?

What (if anything) does it make you want to do?

❸ How does Christ's suffering help you think about your own suffering?

Do you think we can ever suffer more than he did? Why or why not?

He's Alive!
John 20:1-18

They said to her, "Woman, why are you weeping?" She said to them, "They have taken away my Lord, and I do not know where they have laid him." When she had said this, she turned around and saw Jesus standing there, but she did not know that it was Jesus. Jesus said to her, "Woman, why are you weeping? Whom are you looking for?" Supposing him to be the gardener, she said to him, "Sir, if you have carried him away, tell me where you have laid him, and I will take him away." Jesus said to her, "Mary!" She turned and said to him in Hebrew, "Rabbouni!" (which means Teacher). . . .

Discover
Living
Water

Mary Magdalene went and announced to the disciples, "I have seen the Lord." (John 20:13-16, 18, NRSV)

It has been three days since Jesus was laid in the tomb. But now his body is gone. When Mary discovers the empty tomb, she assumes his body has been stolen. She will soon find out that Jesus walked out on his own.

Of course, not everyone believes that. People have developed theories to prove the Resurrection never happened. One is the swoon theory, which says that Jesus never actually died on the cross; he just fainted. After he was buried and the huge stone was rolled across the tomb, he somehow revived. Then he moved the stone, chased away the Roman guards, and convinced the disciples he had risen from the dead.

A second theory suggests the disciples and Mary were in such grief that they were having hallucinations and just thought

Jesus was alive. When we read about Thomas in the next chapter, this theory becomes difficult to support.

The most widely circulated theory is the stolen body theory, which says the disciples stole Jesus' body out of the tomb and made up the story of the Resurrection. If this theory is true, we are left with a puzzling question. All of the disciples were persecuted or killed for their belief in the resurrection of Jesus. If the Resurrection were a lie, why would they die for a lie?

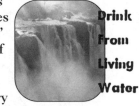

Drink
From
Living
Water

We are left looking at the evidence, trying to determine for ourselves what actually happened. Upcoming chapters reveal that people had separate encounters with the risen Lord. Were they all in on a conspiracy? If so, how did they collaborate on such an elaborate plot?

The body was never found. It was stolen, hidden, or raised from the dead. Jesus' empty grave forces us to decide whether or not we believe in the Resurrection. Our conclusion will determine our faith.

Without the Resurrection, Christianity preaches a prophet and teacher who taught us how to live. With the Resurrection, Christianity preaches a Savior who comes into our life as Lord. Only one has the power to change your life. He is the one who's talked about in this passage. And he is no longer dead.

He's alive!

Dive Into Living Water

① What is the most compelling piece of evidence for you that Jesus rose from the dead? Why?

② How does Mary recognize Jesus?

What does he say to her?

③ What impact does Jesus' resurrection have on your faith?

Is belief in Jesus' resurrection important for our faith? How would our faith be different if Jesus had died on the cross for us—and stayed dead?

The Need for Evidence
John 20:19-31

Now Thomas (called Didymus), one of the Twelve, was not with the disciples when Jesus came. So the other disciples told him, "We have seen the Lord!" But he said to them, "Unless I see the nail marks in his hands and put my finger where the nails were, and put my hand into his side, I will not believe it." A week later his disciples were in the house again, and Thomas was with them. Though the doors were locked, Jesus came and stood among them and said, "Peace be with you!" Then he said to Thomas, "Put your finger here; see my hands. Reach out your hand and put it into my side. Stop doubting and believe." Thomas said to him, "My Lord and my God!" Then Jesus told him, "Because you have seen me, you have believed; blessed are those who have not seen and yet have believed." (John 20:24-29, NIV)

Discover Living Water

Imagine yourself in Thomas' shoes. You have been staying with the other disciples since Jesus died. One night you have to run an errand; when you come back, your friends look like they've seen a ghost. They run up to you and start talking all at once. They are talking so fast you can't understand them. Finally they slow down enough so you can hear their words: "We have seen the Lord" (verse 24)!

You are shocked. You wonder if they could be hallucinating. Maybe they missed Jesus so much that they just imagined he was there. He couldn't have actually been there, could he?

You wish you had never left so you could have seen for yourself what really happened. You want to believe your friends. But unless you see Jesus with your own eyes and touch his wounds with your own hands, you won't be able to believe. You decide to stay with your friends even though you feel a little alienated from them. Although you would never admit it, part of you secretly hopes Jesus will show up again.

Drink From Living Water

One week later, he does. This time he walks directly up to you. Jesus takes your finger and puts it first in his hands, then in his side. You feel the wounds. You look into his eyes. You know without a doubt that the Jesus you knew and the Jesus you're seeing now are one and the same. So you bow down to worship him. You are both ashamed and grateful that you needed this kind of proof. But you no longer doubt.

Little do you know that from

that moment on, people will refer to you as "Doubting Thomas," all because you needed to see Jesus for yourself. You hope that someday people who have doubts will be encouraged by your story. You also hope they will stick with their friends who believe in Jesus until they experience him for themselves.

Sooner or later, Jesus will show up. Then the doubting will stop and faith will take its place.

① How much are you like Thomas?

Dive
Into
Living
Water

Do you tend to believe what you hear—or not?

② Why do you think it was so important for Thomas to touch Jesus' wounds?

③ How does Thomas' experience with Jesus affect his faith?

How does it affect yours?

Resurrection Meal
John 21:1–14

Early in the morning, Jesus stood on the shore, but the disciples did not realize that it was Jesus. He called out to them, "Friends, haven't you any fish?" "No," they answered. He said, "Throw your net on the right side of the boat and you will find some." When they did, they were unable to haul the net in because of the large number of fish. Then the disciple whom Jesus loved said to Peter, "It is the Lord!" As soon as Simon Peter heard him say, "It is the Lord," he wrapped his outer garment around him (for he had taken it off) and jumped into the water. ...

Jesus said to them, "Come and have breakfast." None of the disciples dared ask him, "Who are you?" They knew it was the Lord. (John 21:4-7, 12, NIV)

Discover Living Water

The disciples are fishing again. They had dropped everything to follow Jesus, but now he is gone. They knew he was alive—they had seen him; but they didn't know if they would see him again. Maybe they are beginning to wonder if it was really him they saw. So they go back to doing what they know how to do. And Jesus meets them right there.

They haven't caught any fish when they hear a voice cry, "Throw your net on the right side" (verse 6). Peter must have remembered the time Jesus made a similar suggestion (Luke 5:4). Maybe he got that melancholy feeling you get when you are reminded of someone you miss. This time Peter doesn't argue. He and the disciples just do what they are told.

That's when *déjà vu* sets in. Have you ever experienced

that? You're doing something, and suddenly you have this strange sense you have been there before. That must have been how the disciples felt when they pulled in all those fish. One of the disciples finally shouts out what they're probably all thinking, "It is the Lord!" (verse 7).

Drink From Living Water

Now it's Peter's turn for *déjà vu*. The last time they saw Jesus from their boat, Peter walked on water to get to him (Matthew 14:28). This time he just swims. (Maybe he's a little less confident after the whole denial episode.) Jesus welcomes his disciples by making a little breakfast. In doing so, he builds their confidence that he's really alive.

When we need to see God, we

106

should go back to where we have seen God before. Sometimes it's a physical place. For the disciples, it was their fishing boat. Sometimes we need to travel, not to a place—but to a memory—to experience God's presence. Reliving that memory helps us know the God who was with us then is with us now, even if we can't see it.

Then, just when we least expect it, we experience God again. That's what happened to the disciples. It was a breakfast they'll never forget.

① Why do you think Jesus appears to the disciples in this way?

What does that show you about Jesus?

② Verse 12 says none of the disciples asks Jesus who he is. How do you think they know?

What clues do they have?

③ What would it be like for you to have breakfast with Jesus?

What would you bring (if anything)?

Feed My Sheep

John 21:15–25

When they had finished eating, Jesus said to Simon Peter, "Simon son of John, do you truly love me more than these?" "Yes, Lord," he said, "you know that I love you." Jesus said, "Feed my lambs." Again Jesus said, "Simon son of John, do you truly love me?" He answered, "Yes, Lord, you know that I love you." Jesus said, "Take care of my sheep." The third time he said to him, "Simon son of John, do you love me?" Peter was hurt because Jesus asked him the third time, "Do you love me?" He said, "Lord, you know all things; you know that I love you." Jesus said, "Feed my sheep. I tell you the truth, when you were younger you dressed yourself and went where you wanted; but when you are old you will stretch out your hands, and someone else will dress you and lead you where you do not want to go." (John 21:15-18, NIV)

Discover Living Water

In the final chapter of John we find Jesus talking to Peter—the man who denied him a few days ago. But this is also the man who jumped out of the boat to meet him a few minutes ago. In a way, Peter's faith is like our own—and that's why it's reassuring that Jesus' last words are to him.

The first time Jesus asks Peter if he loves him, Jesus says, "Do you truly love me more than these" (verse 15)? They are eating fish, so it appears Jesus is asking if Peter loves him more than fish. That seems like an odd thing to ask until we think about Peter's life. Catching fish was his livelihood. So what Jesus is really asking is, "Peter, what place do I have in your life?"

Two more times Jesus asks Peter if he loves him. Peter says three times that he does. Peter's three denials have been replaced by three affirmations of love. Each time Jesus tells Peter the same thing: "Feed my sheep."

Peter is told by Jesus that feeding sheep will include being led where he may not want to go (verse 18).

Drink From Living Water

Jesus lets Peter know he'll be with him because he says, "Follow me" (verse 19). He doesn't expect Peter to go there on his own.

Later in the passage, Peter wants to know about the other disciples and where they'll be going. He points to one of them and asks, "What about him" (verse 21)? Jesus' answer in verse 22 lets Peter know that he will only know his own story.

The other disciple's story is not Peter's concern.

It reminds me of a scene from "The Horse and His Boy," one of C. S. Lewis' books in *The Chronicles of Narnia*. A boy named Shasta meets Aslan the Lion for the very first time. Aslan retraces Shasta's life and shows him why everything has happened to him. But Shasta doesn't just want to hear about his own life. He has a friend named Aravis, and he has questions about her life too. When he asks Aslan, Aslan says, "I am telling you your story, not hers. I tell no one any story but his own."

Aslan's words are similar to Jesus' words in verse 22—and they're good words for us to hear too. Each of us has a story—and it will be unlike anyone else's in the world. That's why it is so important for us to live it.

❶ Why do you think Jesus made a point of asking Peter three times if he loved him?

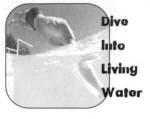

Dive Into Living Water

What does that tell you about Jesus?

❷ What does loving Jesus have to do with feeding sheep?

Why is it so important for Jesus to ask Peter if he loved him before he told him to feed his sheep?

❸ How do you think Jesus wants you to feed his sheep?

What gifts and abilities have you been given that you could use to serve God?